GOD THE CENTER OF VALUE

H. Richard Niebuhr

GOD
The CENTER Of VALUE ❧

Value Theory in the
Theology *of* H. Richard
NIEBUHR

By
C. DAVID GRANT

TEXAS CHRISTIAN UNIVERSITY PRESS
FORT WORTH

Quotations from the unpublished manuscripts of H. Richard Niebuhr used by permission of Richard R. Niebuhr on behalf of Florence M. Niebuhr.

Frontispiece of H. Richard Niebuhr by Richard R. Niebuhr. Used by permission.

Library of Congress Cataloging in Publication Data

Grant, C. David, 1949–
  God the center of value.

  Bibliography: p.
  Includes index.
  1. Niebuhr, H. Richard (Helmut Richard), 1894–1962. 2. Christian ethics—History—20th century. 3. God—History of doctrines—20th century. 4. Values—History—20th century. I. Title.
BX4827.N47G73 1984 230'.5734'0924 84-40232
ISBN 0-87565-227-1 (pbk.)

Designed by
Whitehead & Whitehead • Austin

Contents

I heard upon his dry dung heap
That man cry out who cannot sleep:
"If God is God He is not good,
If God is good He is not God;
Take the even, take the odd. . . ."

Archibald MacLeish, *J. B.*

Preface

I HAVE FOR SEVERAL YEARS been fascinated by the phenomenon of faith. That fascination led me first to study my own religious tradition, for "faith" at that time in my life meant "Christian faith." While pursuing this study, I came under the influence of Schubert M. Ogden of Southern Methodist University, who helped me see that the problem of faith is larger than any one religious tradition. It is a human problem that all of us, whether participants in a religious tradition or not, must confront.

In those early years of my graduate study, I had already begun to sense that faith was closely related to the issue of value, and I found Protestant liberalism with its emphasis on morality and practical reason most attractive. Yet all of us theologically nurtured in the 1960s and '70s were made only too aware of the failing and faults of liberalism by the then-still-strong voices of neo-orthodoxy.

H. Richard Niebuhr came as a happy discovery to me in my first year of doctoral studies at Harvard University. I shall never forget reading *Radical Monotheism and Western Culture* for the first time; my now-worn copy still contains my exuberant marginalia. For here was someone who, like the liberals, understood faith valuationally, but who seemed to avoid many of the pitfalls that had entrapped them. That discovery led me over the years to thoroughly research Niebuhr's thought. The result of that research is presently before the reader.

One's ideas grow and develop out of one's relations with others. I could not begin to acknowledge all who have decisively shaped my thinking. Let me therefore simply thank those who have had a direct hand in the actual production of this work. William M. Longsworth was the first to read sections of the manuscript. His encouragement and high standards were invaluable in the early going. Richard R. Niebuhr of Harvard Divinity School graciously gave me access to much of his father's manuscript material. Gordon D. Kaufman, also of Harvard, carefully read early versions of this study and offered insightful suggestions for improving the argument and encouragement along the way. But most of all I want to thank my wife, Deborah, who typed significant portions of the manuscript. With her hands, she has made an indispensable contribution to this project; with her love, an indispensable contribution to my life.

A word about gender-specific pronouns is in order. In the following pages I have tried to avoid the use of gender-specific pronouns in cases where the antecedent's gender is unspecified, because, among other reasons, H. Richard Niebuhr has helped me see that language, like all of life, is in history and that the meanings of words are fluid. We live in a socio-historical culture in which the use of masculine pronouns to refer to indefinite antecedents is awkward to many and offensive to some. But finding a suitable alternative is difficult. I have tried to avoid such constructions. However, in those places where a singular gender-indefinite antecedent remains, I have chosen to employ "they" and its inflections, preferring this to the more awkward "he or she." Precedent for such usage can be found in no less of an authority than the Oxford English Dictionary. I therefore ask my readers to keep in mind when they come upon a use of "they" with a singular antecedent, that it so appears by conscious intention and not by unconscious blunder.

Fort Worth, Texas
March, 1984

To my brother, Chuck

CHAPTER ONE

Introduction

I N THE HISTORY of the Judeo-Christian tradition, discourse about God—both cultic and theological—has involved language of both being and value. For example, in the so-called "P" account of creation (Genesis 1:1–2:4a), God is seen as the very source of existing reality ("Let there be . . . . And there was. . . . ") as well as the very source of creation's value ("And God saw that it was good"). Much later, in the Middle Ages, Thomas Aquinas opens his *Summa Theologica* with his well-known Five Ways to prove the existence (i.e., the being) of God. Following his discussion of these Five Ways he asks, "Whether goodness and being are the same reality?" and concludes that they are.[1] Aquinas thus holds God to be both First Cause and *Summum Bonum*.

This double attribution to God of being and value has taken on heightened significance in Christian theology since the eighteenth century, due primarily to the impact of Immanuel Kant's work. In the "Transcedental Dialectic" of his *Critique of Pure Reason* Kant made a devastating attack on the theretofore generally accepted arguments for the existence of God, all of which Kant took to rest on the fallacious predication of existence to the concept of the *ens realissimum*. For the theoretical reason, the *idea* of God had important regulative functions; nevertheless the theoretical reason was mistaken, according to Kant, when it took that idea as a *real* being. Kant did find a way to speak of the reality of

God, only it was from the realm of moral values—in Kant's terms, the realm of practical reason—rather than from the realm of theoretical reason. Kant's own argument for God's reality is based on the practical necessity of the postulate of God to make human moral experience intelligible.

In Protestant Christian theology much of the work of the nineteenth century focused on this Kantian issue of the moral reality of God. Albrecht Ritschl, perhaps the most influential theologian of Protestant liberalism, proposed to identify religious statements entirely with what he called value-judgments: statements about God were interpreted, not as ontological claims about God's reality independent of the believer, but rather as valuational claims about the value of God to the believer. Valuational language about God was held to be an entirely different realm of discourse from the language used to describe the being of objects in the world.

Helmut Richard Niebuhr (1894–1962) was an American theologian whose work was decisively shaped by the liberals' valuational approach to theological language. His mentor during his graduate study at Yale was the American liberal theologian Douglas Clyde Macintosh. Ernst Troeltsch, a prominent representative of the branch of German liberalism known as the *religionsgeschichtliche Schule*, served as the focus for Niebuhr's own doctoral dissertation. However, in the 1930s Niebuhr came to reject much of what he had earlier accepted in liberalism, due to the increasing influence that European dialectical theology had upon him. Yet his rejection was not total. Many of the themes that had early aroused his interest in liberal theology remained, though transformed, in his post-liberal thought. Historical relativism was one of those themes; the issue of value was another.

The following study investigates Niebuhr's view of value and his conception of its role in theology. Niebuhr's work is especially fruitful with regard to the issue of value and theology, for he was one of the few theologians in the contemporary period to address philosophical issues in the theory of value and yet relate explicitly such issues to his own understanding of God.

The question that directs the following investigation is, How does Niebuhr's theory of value relate to his theology? The thesis to be argued is that his theory of value constitutes one of two moments within his discussion of value. Though his philosophical theory of value as a phenomenological description of value is intelligible apart from theological considerations, within his thought as a whole it functions critically to relativize all human finite values: God is viewed in his value theory as a critical relativizing principle. The second moment in his discussion is his theology of value, in which the religious experience of being valued by God transforms the theory so that it functions more positively: God becomes the Absolute Valuer. The theory as transformed by the theology serves to define the attitude of confidence and humility with which relative value judgments should be made. Thus Niebuhr's discussion of value moves in two directions. On the one hand, it moves upward from an analysis of the phenomenon of value to the theological implications contained therein; on the other, it moves from God's valuing of the self downward to the implications of that primary valuation for the relative valuations of the self in its world.

Methodologically, this suggests that despite his continual denials to be anything other than a confessional theologian of the church, Niebuhr's analysis arises simultaneously from two directions: from human experience in general and from confessional experience in particular. This double movement within his thought is the source of many creative tensions as well as confusing ambiguities.

In the following analysis, more attention is focused on the movement in Niebuhr's thought from human phenomena to theological implications than on the movement from confessional theology downward. This is due in part, no doubt, to my own theological predilections. But it is also a result of

3

my coming to see how critically central Niebuhr's own sociological, phenomenological, and philosophical presuppositions are in his theory of value as well as in his theology. I
try to raise these presuppositions, so often an undercurrent
in his thought, to an observable level. I hope that heuristi-
cally this focus will prove informative to the reader.

CHAPTER TWO

Confessionalism and Philosophy in Niebuhr's Thought

ALUE THEORY plays a crucial role in H. Richard Niebuhr's theology and ethics. For many of his neo-orthodox contemporaries, value theory was an often ignored if not explicitly rejected way of gaining insight into the nature of theology and that of which theology speaks. Niebuhr, however, accepted the idea of value with open arms as an indispensable tool in his quest to describe and criticize the life of faith. Yet he did so fully aware that the complete reduction of theology and the language of faith to the language of value is as serious a mistake as the refusal to employ value theory in theology at all. Niebuhr's many discussions of value and value theory, from his programmatic 1937 essay "Value-Theory and Theology" to the two draft chapters of his unfinished *magnum opus* on Christian ethics left on his desk at his death in 1962,[1] consistently view the development of a theory of value as an important prerequisite for an adequate interpretation of faith, religion, and theology.

Our first task in this study is to examine Niebuhr's theory of value as a philosophical theory. Such an approach must be taken with care, for it risks the misinterpretation that Niebuhr's theory of value is independent of his theology, that God and value are intelligible apart from each other—a claim the denial of which is one of Niebuhr's important contributions to twentieth-century theology. Another danger in such an approach is inappropriately to compare Niebuhr

5

with major philosophical value theorists of his time. Niebuhr's own work in value theory was but a part of his theological and ethical concerns, and his brief forays into the issues of value theory are more suggestive than thoroughly and carefully worked out. Niebuhr was certainly well-familiar with the writings of his contemporaries in the philosophy of value, and he often took a critical stance toward their work.[2] Yet to take his brief essay, "The Center of Value," and place it against, say, R. B. Perry's *General Theory of Value* or C. I. Lewis's *Analysis of Knowledge and Valuation*, is to make an unfair comparison. Nevertheless, an examination of his value theory on philosophical grounds will help clarify key concepts and patterns of argument in his thought as a whole and will lay a basis from which to examine the further question of the relation between his value theory and his conception of God.

Is such a philosophical approach to his value theory appropriate to the spirit of his own work? As James Gustafson notes, "It would be unfair to Niebuhr to cast him in an intellectual role he did not intend to play."[3] Niebuhr held a long-standing conviction that theology must be "resolutely confessional"[4] and stated late in his life that "my primary concern today . . . is still that of the reformation of the church."[5] In light of this statement it must be asked whether a philosophical examination of Niebuhr's value theory is liable to Gustafson's criticism. Two important related aspects of Niebuhr's thought—the meaning of his claim that theology must be resolutely confessional and the role that philosophy plays in his own theology and ethics—show that it is not and that a philosophical approach to Niebuhr's thought is appropriate.

1. NIEBUHR'S EPISTEMOLOGICAL CONFESSIONALISM

Niebuhr's claim that theology must be confessional is misinterpreted, if "confessional" is taken to mean only what it has meant for most other twentieth-century theologians. For the German theologians involved in the Confessional Church that arose in opposition to the Nazi-supported German-Christians during World War II, "confessional" had primary reference to their loyalty to the Augsburg Confession and other confessions of the Reformation.[6] Karl Barth, the theologian most often associated with confessional theology in this century, also employs the term in this ecclesiological or creedal sense. For him, "the confessional attitude of dogmatics and Church proclamation means fidelity as required by the Word of God to the fathers and the confession of the Churches as the voice of those who were in the Church before us."[7] Though Niebuhr held "the voice of those who were in the Church before us" in high esteem in his own thinking, his confessionalism does not refer only to this aspect of his thought.[8] Its more primary root is epistemological; that theology must be confessional is but a corollary of Niebuhr's contention that whatever we know is known only from our own particular standpoint.

Niebuhr works out the basis for his confessional theology in his first major constructive book, *The Meaning of Revelation*, published in 1941. In its first chapters he sets out more clearly than elsewhere the epistemological position undergirding the whole of his thought. It is also the only major work in which Niebuhr describes his theology as confessional.[9]

Niebuhr begins this book by examining historical relativism. This issue plays a central role in his thinking as a result of his early exposure to Ernst Troeltsch (which culminated in his doctoral thesis "Ernst Troeltsch's Philosophy of Religion")[10] and is an underlying preoccupation of his first two published books, *The Social Sources of Denominationalism* (1929) and *The Kingdom of God in America* (1937). Both books are descriptive analyses—one primarily sociological and the other primarily historical—of the phenomena of American Christianity. In the first book Niebuhr is capti-

7

vated by the overwhelming diversity of denominations in America, finally attributing their differences not to creedal and theological beliefs but to "the cultural and political conditions prevailing in any group of Christians."[11] In *The Kingdom of God in America* he seeks a unifying factor in all the diverse denominations and finds it in their common acceptance of the idea of the Kingdom of God as central.[12] Yet even in his search for a unifying factor, the diversity of historical phenomena is fully acknowledged. For the pattern of unity which Niebuhr seeks in the idea of the Kingdom of God is sought in hopes that it might "illustrate something of the significance of Christianity as a universal faith which *must nevertheless take on particular historical and relative character.*"[13]

The position Niebuhr develops in *The Meaning of Revelation* can be seen as his attempt to work out an epistemology that can support the validity and meaningfulness of religious language while yet recognizing to the fullest extent the historical relativity of that language. "We are aware today," says Niebuhr in his preface to this book,

> that all our philosophical ideas, religious dogmas and moral imperatives are historically conditioned and this awareness tempts us to a new agnosticism. I have found myself unable to avoid the acceptance of historical relativism yet I do not believe that the agnostic consequence is necessary. Such relativism calls rather, I believe, for the development of a new type of critical idealism which recognizes the social and historical character of the mind's categories and is "belieffully" realistic, in Professor Tillich's meaning of that phrase.[14]

In the opening chapters of the book he sketches the major lines of just such a critical idealism.

Niebuhr's epistemological position is basically Kantian. Knowing is never simply a reading-off of facts from objective realities, although there is an objective component in it.

8

With Kant, Niebuhr seeks a mediating position that incorporates the affirmations of both realism and idealism while yet rejecting their denials of each other. Such a position recognizes that the mind brings to its experience of objective realities its own structures, categories, and schemata. As a result, our experience of and reflection on those objective realities is as much the product of the interpreting structures of our minds as it is of the objects' sensory impact.

However, Niebuhr's epistemological position differs significantly from Kant's at two points. For Kant the categories, forms of intuition, and schemata which the mind brings to experience are structures of *universal* human reason. Though it is "solely from the human standpoint" that, according to Kant, we can speak of our experience of objects, nevertheless that human standpoint is shared in common by all:

> What objects may be in themselves, and apart from all this receptivity of our sensibility, remains completely unknown to us. We know nothing but our mode of perceiving them—a mode which is peculiar to us, and not necessarily shared in by every being, *though, certainly, by every human being.*[15]

Niebuhr rejects Kant's assumption that we can meaningfully speak of such a common human reason. Niebuhr therefore takes Kant's *Critique* a step further than does Kant himself; Niebuhr thinks we must examine the transcendental grounds not only of human reason in general but also of the various concrete historical manifestations of that reason. Hence the most we can speak of is human reason as it occurs in a particular society:

> We are . . . beings whose concepts are something less than the categories of a universal reason. Critical idealists knew themselves to be human selves with a specific

9

psychological and logical equipment; their successors know themselves to be social human beings whose reason is not a common reason, alike in all human selves, but one which is qualified by inheritance from a particular society.[16]

Understanding how reason operates will thus always entail understanding how some particular historic reason operates.

The categories of the social mind reside in the language of socio-historical groups. The particular "patterns of interpretation," "images," and "symbols" carried in the "common memory" function in Niebuhr's scheme much like the categories of pure reason function in Kant's: they provide the mental structures necessary for the possibility of experiencing, and hence having knowledge of, anything at all. The individual takes up these social patterns, images, and symbols in the process of socialization. They are

> the product . . . of a society which has taught [the self] a language with names and explicit or implicit metaphors and with an implicit logic. With the aid of that language the self has learned to divide up the continuum of its experiences into separate entities, to distinguish things and persons, processes in nature and movements in society.[17]

By learning the language of their society, individuals implicitly take on the historic reason of that society.

By "language" Niebuhr intends a meaning richer than what is intended when one speaks of the English "language" or the German "language." A language is relative to a socio-historical group and is the carrier of meanings within such a group. Though several such groups might well share outwardly in the same native tongue, each would have its own language with its particular patterns of interpretation, images, and symbols. Hence Niebuhr can speak of the common mind of the Christian community and refer to a historical movement that transcends the many native tongues of those who have participated in that movement.

Yet the point of view from which we apprehend the objects about us is not determined solely by the socio-historical community of which we are a part. It is also determined by the mode of understanding with we which approach those objects—that of the impersonal, objective, theoretical reason or that of the personal, subjective, practical reason. (Here again we see the influence of Kant.) Each individual in a particular socio-cultural stream views reality personally at times, and, at other times, impersonally. Some aspects of that reality are best understood by the personal mode; some, by the impersonal mode; others need to be understood through both modes. Yet as integrally related as they are in the one self, these modes stand independent of each other.

In *The Meaning of Revelation* Niebuhr distinguishes between these modes of understanding as they are employed in our knowledge of history. The impersonal, objectifying, theoretical reason when applied to history results in what Niebuhr calls "external history"; the personal, subjective, practical reason when so applied results in "internal history." The most helpful distinction he makes between these two histories takes the form of an illustration:

> Of a man who has been blind and who has come to see, two histories can be written. A scientific case history will describe what happened to his optic nerve or to the crystaline lens, what technique the surgeon used or by what medicines a physician wrought the cure, through what stages of recovery the patient passed. An autobiography, on the other hand, may barely mention these things but it will tell what happened to a self that had lived in darkness and now saw again trees and the sunrise, children's faces and the eyes of a friend.[18]

At stake in this illustration of the differing perspectives are not the different locational vantage points of the surgeon and the patient. Obviously the patient could never directly perceive the techniques employed in the surgery performed on his own eyes, nor could the surgeon experience the patient's visual restoration. Rather, at stake in the illustration are different ways of understanding the event, available to some degree to both patient and surgeon. The patient could himself be a surgeon, or at least someone knowledgeable concerning surgical procedures and optic anatomy, and be able to converse with his doctors about the procedure in all its technical complexities. Likewise, the surgeon performing the operation could relate personally to the patient's joys and excitement by remembering times in the surgeon's own personal life when the intensity and newness of a visual experience were overwhelmingly joyful. Hence both surgeon and patient could approach the restoration of sight by means of each of these modes of understanding, though certainly the impersonal mode, for a surgeon, and the personal mode, for a patient, would remain primary.

Niebuhr employs a type of faculty psychology to distinguish further these two modes of understanding. Two faculties are shared by the impersonal and personal modes—imagination and reason. These two modes are distinguished by the faculty that supplies the raw data on which reason and imagination in turn operate. In the objective, impersonal mode *sensation* supplies the data; in the subjective, personal mode it is *affection*.

External, objective, impersonal knowledge begins with perceptual sensations that arise from the five senses. However, this "jostling mob of confused, unintelligible, meaningless, visual and auditory sensations" is useless in its raw state. Those sensations must be made "to march in order by a mind which approaches and apprehends them with some total image."[19] That image is supplied by what Niebuhr calls the imagination:

We hasten to meet the sensations that come to us with

anticipations of our own. We do not hear isolated ejacu-
lations, separate and therefore meaningless words but
apprehend each sound in a context that we in part supply. By means of ideas we interpret as we sense, and
sense as we interpret. We anticipate connections between sensations before they are given and through
imagination supply what is lacking in the immediate
datum. So we may apprehend the meaning of a brown,
rough texture of certain size and shape as the bark of a
tree, or as a tree, or even as an experience of the adap-
tation of life to its environment. In such knowing of
things everything depends upon the continuous conversation between sensation and imagination.[20]

Yet sometimes the imagination leads us astray in our
knowledge of the external world when it uses the wrong
images, wrong patterns, or wrong ideas in its attempt to get
the jumbled input of sensations "to march in order." "We
are not easily deceived," says Niebuhr, "by sensation but are
fooled by a false imagination which interprets some sense-
datum as part of a whole context to which it does not belong." Further developing the example of perceiving a tree,
he continues: "In the darkness a perverse imagination interprets the visual impression of one side and section of the
tree trunk so as to make a ghost out of the whole; in a moment of inattention I accept the word 'bark' as part of a sentence about a dog rather than about a tree." When such mistakes occur, reason is employed as the faculty that corrects
the imagination: "Reason does not dispense with imagination but seeks to employ apt images and patterns whereby
an otherwise inscrutable sensation becomes a true symbol of
a reality whose other aspects, as anticipated in the image,
are available to common experience."[21] Such repeated, critical, and common experience is available in the community
of knowers who commonly have before them the object
which is known.

A similar relationship exists among the three faculties in

the personal mode of understanding. Imagination again supplies images and patterns that order chaotic and varied raw data into a whole; but in this mode of understanding the raw data is supplied by affections:

> Pain and pleasure here are not physical states primarily; what is important about them is that they are *ours*; they occur in *our* bodies, directly or sympathetically, and so become joys and sorrows of the self; they are states of the soul. Nothing happens without the participation of our bodies, but the affections of the soul come to us through and in our social body almost as much as in our individual structure. We suffer with and in our community and there we also rejoice. With joys and sorrows, fears, hopes, loves, hates, pride, humility and anger combine. And none of these affections remains uninterpreted. We meet each one with an imagination whereby we supply what is lacking in the immediate datum and are enabled to respond, rightly or wrongly, to a whole of reality of which this affection is for us a symbol and a part.[22]

Reason again functions in a corrective role, only here it corrects the evil imaginations of the heart that arise in the mind's attempt to order the affections of the soul. Unlike many who emphasize the dimension of the affective and emotional, Niebuhr constantly calls for the operation of reason in this sphere. Reason for him is not limited to the objective, nor imagination to the subjective mode; both faculties operate in both modes. Hence there is no "choice between reason and imagination but only between reasoning on the basis of adequate images and thinking with the aid of evil imaginations."[23]

Niebuhr appeals to a pragmatic criterion to indicate how the reason distinguishes between evil imaginations and adequate images in the personal mode of understanding. Reason judges the images according to their ability to bring order and wholeness to the chaotic jumble of affections. "Evil imaginations," says Niebuhr, "are shown to be evil by their consequences to selves and communities just as erroneous concepts and hypotheses in external knowledge are shown to be fallacious by their results."[24] The source of many modern evil imaginations is our attempt "to employ in the understanding of personal relations the images which we have learned to use with some success in our external, non-participating knowledge of things."[25] Such an attempt constitutes what Gilbert Ryle has called a category-mistake, in which one uses, in Niebuhr's terms, an image appropriate and apt for the impersonal objective mode of reason for a completely different mode of understanding.[26] For though the imagination works similarly in both the personal and impersonal modes of understanding, Niebuhr seems to imply that the images brought to bear on the sensations, on the one hand, and the affections, on the other, are themselves of disparate source and content. Such a move enables Niebuhr to locate revelation—which is, after all, his ultimate interest in discussing epistemology—as the source of the images with which we come to our affections:

> Whatever else revelation means it does mean an event in our history which brings rationality and wholeness into the confused joys and sorrows of personal existence and allows us to discern order in the brawl of communal histories. Such revelation is no substitute for reason; the illumination it supplies does not excuse the mind from labor; but it does give to that mind the impulsion and the first principles it requires if it is to be able to do its proper work. In this sense we may say that the revelatory moment is revelatory because it is rational, because it makes the understanding of order and meaning in personal history possible.[27]

Whence arise the affections that provide the raw data for the personal mode of understanding? Niebuhr views the functioning of the two modes of understanding as closely parallel, with three corresponding faculties in each of the modes. The affections therefore arise, as do the sensations in the theoretical, objective, impersonal mode of understanding, from the relation of the knower to a reality independent of the knower. Only, in the case of the personal mode what gives rise to the affections is not a relation to sensible things but to a different kind of reality—selves and the matters that surround the life of selves, or in short, the world of values.

Perhaps Niebuhr's strongest appeal for the objectivity of that which gives rise to the affections is contained in his third Cole Lecture delivered at Vanderbilt University in 1960, entitled "Towards the Recovery of Feeling." Niebuhr there parallels our current suspicion of the reality of the objects of the emotional life with the ancient Greeks' suspicion of the reality of the objects of the senses. The ever-changing sensible world was for them, he reminds us, "the realm of mere opinion, of *doxa*, of the transitory, the unreliable, the illusory." [28] In contrast, the realm of reason, of the forms, was the only reliable source of knowledge. In a similar way, so he says, we now distrust the reality of the emotions and find true knowledge only in the theoretical, observing, impersonal reason of the sciences. But Niebuhr calls us back to an engagement with the emotional life, for it is his belief that the emotions "put us into touch with what is reliable, firm, real, enduring in ways that are inaccessible to the conceptual and spectator reason." [29]

The objectivity of emotional experience and of the independent realities that give rise to the emotions is the second point at which Niebuhr's epistemological program differs from Kant's.

For Kant, the *sensibility* receives "representations through the mode in which we are affected by objects" [30] and the *understanding* applies concepts to the intuitions, thereby organizing the raw data received. *Reason* in turn provides unity to the manifold knowledge in the understanding, just as understanding provides unity by means of its concepts to the manifold of intuitions received by sensibility. Reason does so by means of "transcendental ideas," which neither extend nor supplement the knowledge gained by understanding but merely provide the conditions for the possibility of a unified integration of knowledge. This point is important, for it means that "reason never applies itself directly to experience or to any object, but to understanding."[31] Rather, these ideas of reason—chief among which Kant has in mind the ideas of self, world, and God—function regulatively:

> I . . . maintain that transcendental ideas . . . have an excellent, and indeed indispensably necessary, regulative employment, namely, that of directing the understanding towards a certain goal upon which the routes marked out by all its rules converge, as upon their point of intersection. This point is indeed a mere idea, a *focus imaginarius*, from which, since it lies quite outside the bounds of possible experience, the concepts of the understanding do not in reality proceed; none the less it serves to give to these concepts the greatest [possible] unity combined with the greatest [possible] extension.[32]

Problems accrue when we mistakenly take these regulative ideas of reason to be concepts of the understanding, for then we begin to treat God, self, and world as objective realities. But Kant denies in his *Critique of Pure Reason* that we have any grounds to do so. These ideas play an important role in regulating the whole of our knowing but do not apply constitutively to realities that we experience.

Kant does develop in his *Critique of Practical Reason* a way of talking about the objective reality of the transcendental ideas of freedom, immortality of the soul, and God. But their reality independent of the thinker's mind is of a completely different character from the objective reality that Kant gives sensible objects in his first *Critique*, for the reality

17

of the transcendental ideas does not involve the intuitional component so basic to the knowing process in Kant's view of empirical knowledge. Instead, the objective reality of freedom, immortality, and God is founded on their being necessary "postulates of pure practical reason": "By a postulate of pure practical reason, I understand a theoretical proposition which is not as such demonstrable, but which is an inseparable corollary of an a priori unconditionally valid practical law."[33] The law Kant speaks of is the categorical imperative to "so act that the maxim of your will could always hold at the same time as a principle establishing universal law."[34] To make intelligible this demand of the practical reason, the objective reality of freedom, immortality, and God is postulated. But for Kant these are not experienced realities. The reality of the objects of practical reason stems from the logical requirements of reason and not from any receptive faculty that parallels the sensibility.

Niebuhr's view of the objective reality of the objects of practical reason contrasts with Kant's. Niebuhr roots both the personal and impersonal modes of understanding in receptive faculties—sensation and affection. The process by which the mind comes to know realities in the personal sphere, like the process in the impersonal sphere, proceeds by the imagination's application of symbols, patterns of interpretation, ideas and the like to the preconceptually experienced sensations and feelings. Hence for Niebuhr even the objective realities of self and God are mediated to us through a knowing process that has its genesis in realities that stand over against our knowing and reasoning. Niebuhr rarely if ever appeals to any sort of Kantian, transcendentally idealistic conception of the postulated realities of self and God. For him they are realities with which we have at least an indirect contact through the affections. But Niebuhr also holds that our knowledge of these realities is always mediated through inherited symbols and patterns of interpretation, so that we never experience any of these realities as things-in-themselves: "Though an object is independent of a subject, yet it is inaccessible as it is in itself. What is accessible and knowable is so only from a certain point of view and in a certain relation."[35]

Niebuhr's claim that theology must be confessional is therefore best understood as a correlate of his epistemological position that "what is accessible and knowable is so only from a certain point of view and in a certain relation." Since the attainment of any absolute viewpoint is precluded to the human knower, we can only confess that we see things the way we see them from our point of view. Such seeing occurs only with the aid of patterns of interpretation, symbols, and images that we must likewise confess to be relative to the particular socio-historical group of which we find ourselves a part. This is equally true for our knowledge of objective, impersonal realities and for the realities of the personal mode of knowing about which Niebuhr as a theologian is most concerned. Hence Niebuhr's is an epistemological and not simply a creedal confessionalism; far from excluding philosophical considerations, it actually depends on them.

2. THE ROLE OF PHILOSOPHY

If Niebuhr himself employs philosophy as a primary tool in his thought, then a philosophical study of his value theory is not only appropriate; it is necessary. For only such an approach will enable us to judge the adequacy of his use of philosophy.

Of course, much weight rests on the meaning attributed to the word "philosophy." Niebuhr distinguishes two meanings: "philosophy" can be used to refer to the technical, academic discipline, or it can be used "in the quite nontechnical though widely accepted meaning of love of wisdom or understanding."[36] Niebuhr is willing to call himself a philosopher in the latter sense, though he is hesitant to do so in the former. "The love of wisdom," however, is so broad a definition of philosophy as to be almost vacuous; hence his willingness to be called a philosopher in this sense does not really further our understanding the role of philosophy in his thought.

However, when Niebuhr specifies what he means by the love of wisdom, he points to two characteristics that are often used to distinguish philosophy in the technical sense from related disciplines, especially theology. He writes in the prologue to *The Responsible Self*:

> I regard this effort as an essay in Christian moral *philosophy* for two reasons. First, because I am concerned in it in part with the development of an instrument of analysis which applies to any form of human life including the Christian. . . . Secondly, it is more philosophy than theology in the current understanding of theology, because my approach is not Bible-centered, though I think it is Bible-informed. If I dissent from those philosophers who undertake to analyze the moral life as though life were nonhistorical, as though the ideas and words of the English moral language referred to the pure emotions of nonhistorical beings or to pure concepts, I find myself equally ill at ease with theologians who deal with the Scriptures as a nonhistorical book and undertake to explain it as though they were nonhistorical men.[37]

The two characteristics that Niebuhr highlights relate to scope and authority. The scope of the philosopher is more general, more universal than that of the theologian. Theologians seek an analysis of the Christian life and faith. They have before them as their data both the whole history of those who have lived the Christian life and viewed the world by means of Christian patterns of interpretation and symbols, as well as the current lives of Christian believers. Philosophers, on the other hand, focus on the more general questions of the forms of human life and language, seeking in the many and varied manifestations of life and language the patterns and structures inherent in them.

Niebuhr's interest in developing "an instrument of analysis which applies to any form of human life including the Christian" could be seen as inconsistent with his socio-historical relativism, since he continually denies that one can talk of human reason and human experience apart from the particular socio-historical contexts in which they are found: "There is no way of being a religious self as such, any more than there is a way of being a thinking or a feeling or a speaking self as such. I am fated to be these things in the thus-ness and so-ness of my given historicity."[38] Yet what Niebuhr finds valuable in his use of philosophy is not the way that it can uncover a common stratum of human experience and reason but the way that it can analyze the shared forms in which all experience seems to be ensconced. Even in *The Meaning of Revelation*, in which the historicity of experience and reason is most strongly emphasized, Niebuhr tries to show the form and structure in which all knowing comes about. His interest there, as in much of his work, centers on the concrete actuality of the Christian life. Yet he can so focus only after having shown that historicity is a structure shared by all experiencing selves. In his use of philosophy he is not looking for common experience so much as seeking the forms and structures that undergird the many concrete manifestations of human life.

To be sure, there is but a fine distinction between common experience and common structures of experience; Niebuhr himself sometimes failed to make it clearly. Nevertheless the distinction must be made if Niebuhr's thought is to be properly understood.

A helpful analogy clarifying this distinction can be found in the structures of language. Anyone who has studied foreign languages knows that most Indo-European languages have common grammatical structures. Those languages contain words that function as verbs and as nouns, as adjectives and as adverbs. Likewise, sentence structures almost always involve subjects and predicates. One usually learns new languages by taking the basic building blocks—the vocabulary, the declension of nouns, and the conjugation of verbs—and relating these basic structures to the corresponding structures in one's native language. That the basic structures in the languages are shared, however, does not mean that a common human language is shared. Something of an analogous distinction underlies Niebuhr's willingness to investigate the shared structures and forms of human life while yet consistently denying that there is such a thing as "common human experience" or "common human reason."[39]

The second characteristic by which Niebuhr describes his own thought in *The Responsible Self* as more philosophy than theology relates to the question of authority. Niebuhr finds his thought more Bible-informed than Bible-centered, and indeed any reader of Niebuhr will surely agree with that self-assessment. Niebuhr employs Scripture more as a source than as an authority. Scripture provides the images, patterns of interpretation, symbols, and the like by which he as a Christian interprets the reality that confronts him. Theology, as critical reflection on faith, must also allow Scripture to inform the perspective on and in which it reflects. However, theological claims are warranted not by their derivation from Scriptural claims but by the way they successfully interpret as intelligible the life lived by means of those symbols, images, and patterns. Hence though Scripture plays a role in setting the parameters of interpretation, reasoned reflection is the principal tool Niebuhr employs in his attempts to understand faith.

By "reasoned reflection," I refer to Niebuhr's methodological style of approaching problems. Niebuhr is certainly not a rationalist in the strictest sense of the word: he never makes a case for a claim based solely on its rational necessity. Yet he does employ a kind of philosophical procedure, subjecting matters under investigation to reasoned reflection, and hence can be said to be a rationalist in a looser sense of the word.

Niebuhr uses both phenomenological and linguistic methods in his approach. His unpublished manuscript "Faith on Earth" is an excellent example of the former. In this piece, which in part contains chapters later published as *Radical Monotheism and Western Culture*, Niebuhr examines both secular and religious manifestations of the phenomenon of faith in order to find if a common "structure of faith" stands behind those manifestations. He finds such a structure in the relations of trust and loyalty between selves as they stand related to a common third.[40]

Niebuhr's essay "On the Nature of Faith," on the other hand, illustrates his linguistic approach. In a semantic analysis of the word "faith," he carefully sorts out the different uses of the word and the different contexts in which those uses occur. His analysis leads him to collect the meanings of "faith" under two categories: meanings that relate to knowledge and meanings that relate to persons. The conclusion to that article is illustrative, not only of the thrust of the analysis in the article, but also of Niebuhr's rationalism in the looser sense of the word:

> I have thus not elucidated the "nature of faith" but have shown myself to be subject to the "faith" of our times, namely the confidence that analysis will lead to clarification, and that clarification will not end in chaotic pluralism but lead onward to the understanding of how all things hang together in a trustworthy universe, which is the cause of the faithful God.[41]

Niebuhr's confidence that analysis will lead to clarification marks his works as truly philosophical in spirit in more than just the broad sense of philosophy as "love of wisdom." Such a confidence could easily be expressed by many of Niebuhr's contemporaries in philosophy—at least as stated without the final clause, "which is the cause of the faithful God." Hence, though Niebuhr made a distinction between philosophy in a technical sense and philosophy as the love of wisdom, and though he saw himself as a philosopher only in the latter sense, the distinction is not so dichotomous when applied to his own works. His methods are philosophical in the technical sense; the only factors that distinguish him from those to whom he refers as "philosophers" are his willingness to begin his analysis with the concrete data of the Christian life and his unwillingness to seek a universal standpoint from which to reflect on that life. Hence, a philosophical study of Niebuhr's value theory is well-warranted.

CHAPTER THREE

The Nature of Value

NIEBUHR'S THEORY of value constitutes but a part of his overall discussion of ethics. We must begin, then, a study of that theory by examining the general character of his ethics, for his value theory stands integrally related as a part to that larger whole.

1. NIEBUHR'S APPROACH TO ETHICS

Niebuhr's ethical reflections attempt to address the human need to decide about possible courses of action in the world. The intensity with which Niebuhr examines the ethical life arises not out of a speculative fascination with the theoretical issues on which that analysis often pivots but out of his keen awareness that those issues are crucial for the adequate interpretation and criticism of the life lived in responsibility. Niebuhr's discussion of ethics is thus primarily directed to the task of being "an aid in accuracy of action."[1]

Yet Niebuhr's particular way of providing "an aid in accuracy of action" is not to make determinative moral judgments concerning particular ethical dilemmas. Niebuhr rarely makes categorical claims about the rightness of some action or the goodness of some pursued end. Indeed, a frustration in studying Niebuhr's ethics is the paucity of comment he makes revealing his own normative positions.

Niebuhr's published writings contain few works devoted to specific ethical issues. The few that do appear were published before the mid-1940's and address two issues: the problem of industrialization and the labor movement, and the problem of war. The articles on the labor movement appeared before Niebuhr had broken from liberalism. Though they show a definite inclination to associate the labor movement with Christianity, the principles of action proposed are very general and simply delineate the appropriate attitude for the church to take toward the movement. Niebuhr avoids advocating specific actions. In "The Alliance between Labor and Religion" Niebuhr urges that Christianity realign itself with the cause of "the poor in the land"; but rather than giving concrete proposals for action, he concludes by urging the church "to lead the way to the goal by way of the cross."[2] In "Christianity and the Social Problem" he decries the depersonalization that accompanies industrialization and offers three suggestions "how the church [might] apply this social gospel to so un-Christian a situation." One of his suggestions is that "the preaching of the Church might be definite. . . . Cannot the Church seek to be definite in its application of the social gospel to the definite problems?" His other two suggestions focus on the attitude to be taken by the Church in approaching the problems: "Let the application of the social gospel be in the first place *sympathetic*," since "the employer and the employe [*sic*] of today are the results largely of their environment." And secondly, "may the preaching of the social gospel be *Christian*. May it preach the law of sacrifice to employer and employe, but sacrifice not for the sake of present peace. Sacrifice for the attainment of the Kingdom of God." This method of self-sacrifice is "the most effective method at the disposal of the church to hasten the growth of a Christian social order."[3]

Niebuhr's articles addressed to the problem of war focus even more strongly on the delineation of appropriate attitudes. He never suggests that war is good or bad or that pacifist activity is right or wrong for Christians. The action he advocates is not outward at all but is an inner action of the self—repentance—which outwardly appears as inactivity or as "doing nothing." In 1932 Niebuhr contributed an article to *The Christian Century* concerning the then-recent invasion and occupation of Manchuria by the Japanese army. Much of the world community was outraged at the Japanese aggressiveness. Yet Niebuhr counsels Christians to do nothing in either support of or opposition to the Japanese presence. His position is not based on a judgment that the Japanese invasion is either right or wrong, just or unjust, nor that the continued occupation is the best alternative. Rather, it is based "upon the fact that [the Christian's] inability to do anything constructive in the crisis is the inability of one whose own faults are so apparent and so similar to those of the offender that any action on his part is not only likely to be misinterpreted but is also likely—in the nature of the case—to be really less than disinterested." Rather than outward action, "an inactivity then is demanded which will be profoundly active in rigid self-analysis."[4]

Niebuhr's articles concerning World War II reflect the same tendency to focus ethical reflection back upon the attitude of the agent rather than upon the agent's outward actions. Again, Niebuhr is disinclined to make moral judgments on the war or on the ways that it is fought. Indeed, Niebuhr thought discussion of the war in the classic terms of the Just War Theory was "inadequate and misleading."[5] Instead, his suggestions for concrete action focus on how, in view of the war, Christians should re-examine their inner motives and attitudes. In his earliest article on the war, Niebuhr suggests that the war be viewed as the corrective judgment of God. So doing, he concludes, will have "certain consequences for human action":

> The first of these is the abandonment of the habit of passing judgments of our own on ourselves and on our enemies or opponents. . . . A second thing Christians under the judgment of God in war require of themselves, because he requires it of them, is the abandon-

ment of all self-defensiveness, all self-aggrandizement, all thinking in terms of the self as central. . . . Finally, response to God's action in the war is hopeful and trusting response.[6]

In his last article on the war, Niebuhr interprets war in light of the crucifixion and concludes with the following statement of the implications of that interpretation:

> It will be asked, If these suggestions, these vague gestures in the direction of the interpretation of war as crucifixion, are followed, what will be the result for action? No single answer can be given since the cross does not impose a new law on man. But one thing will be common to all actions which are based on such an understanding of war: there will be in them no effort to establish a righteousness of our own, no excusing of self because one has fallen less short of the glory of God than others; there will be no vengeance in them. They will also share one positive characteristic: they will be performed in hope, in reliance on the continued grace of God in the midst of our ungraciousness.[7]

Again, even where Niebuhr addresses a specific moral problem, his conclusions involve not judgments on the rightness of courses of action within those situations but delineations of the appropriate attitude for agents making their own decisions.[8]

How is Niebuhr's interest in the practical use of ethics for the direction of the moral life to be reconciled with his apparent disinclination to provide practical answers to specific issues? Two characteristics of his thought clarify the relation. First, an underlying individualism pervades his ethics, an individualism easily overlooked by the casual reader because of Niebuhr's pervasive talk of the self as social. When he speaks of the self in this way, he tries to draw attention to the strong interconnections between the self's identity and those other selves in community with it. His favorite descriptive image toward this end is that of the triadic relationship between three beings: the self, the social companion, and that third entity which the self and the social companion hold commonly in view. Niebuhr's most familiar application of the triadic model is his analysis of faith, wherein the self and the self's social companion trust and are loyal to each other because of a third reality, the cause, which they commonly share.[9] And not only is the self social in the sense of having its being only in relation to other beings with whom it is presently interconnected, it is social in the sense that it has come to be as the result of a history of social interactions. Hence "to be a self in the presence of other selves is not a derivative experience but primordial."[10]

Yet the social self is nonetheless an individual self. Society never takes on the characteristics of a self in Niebuhr's thought. The chief realities with which Niebuhr deals are individual selves, selves certainly shaped by society but nevertheless shaped as individuals. Though interested in the social communities, he is so only for the sake of providing the context for individuals to understand themselves. Niebuhr is therefore a true "existentialist" in that for him the key to understanding all that is about us rests in understanding our own existences.

Since the brunt of Niebuhr's interest lies in the individual and not in the social realities of which individuals are a part, it is no surprise that when Niebuhr speaks of Christian ethics his focus is on the individual Christian and the decisions that the Christian makes rather than on the development of a normative set of guidelines for "the Christian community." As a self, the Christian exists only within a community of other like-minded selves. Nevertheless, the ethical decisions made by that self are no less that self's own individual decisions because of the communal context. Niebuhr opens his 1952 Christian ethics lectures with the following observation:

No man can tell other people what is right and wrong. Ethics is not law-giving; Leviticus, Exodus, the Sermon on the Mount are not as such our ethics, but merely our guide. Each man must be led to an understanding of what is right and wrong within himself. Criticisms and judgment from others may be a help, but they cannot tell us what is wrong with ourselves.[11]

The personal character of ethics is even more strongly emphasized in his second lecture of that year:

[Ethical] investigation is of course intensely personal; it deals with our selves, our principles, our decisions, our actions. An ethical inquiry is necessarily pursued alone; each of us is on his own. To think it can be done *en masse* is a contradiction in terms. Mass-man is not an ethical concept. If I were to address all 150 of you, I would not be addressing you in your freedom. I would address you in bondage. There is a sense in which I must do this, but that is not my intention. There is a place, I suppose—though I doubt it—for moving masses of people. However, it certainly has no place in ethical inquiry.[12]

Since "no man can tell another what is right and wrong," Niebuhr does not often pronounce moral judgments on specific issues. To do so would be to determine for others decisions that individuals must ultimately make for themselves.[13]

A second characteristic of Niebuhr's ethical thought also explains the lack of specific judgments: his contextualist approach to ethics. Niebuhr was himself unhappy with being called a contextualist,[14] yet the designation describes the way he approaches the ethical task.

Niebuhr's ethics pivots on the idea of responsibility. But for him that idea has to do not so much with accountability as with responsiveness: actions are responsible because "all action, we now say, including what we rather indeterminately call moral action, is response to action upon us." We act, or better, we react according to others' actions. "The idea or pattern of responsibility, then," according to Niebuhr, "may summarily and abstractly be defined as the idea of an agent's action as response to an action upon him in accordance with his interpretation of the latter action and with his expectation of response to his response; and all this is in a continuing community of agents."[15]

For Niebuhr the task of the ethicist is to uncover the context of actions that lead to our responsive action. The Christian ethicist sets forth the overarching, ultimate context in which our action takes place. For Niebuhr this overarching context is God; hence Niebuhr's most central and fundamental ethical principle: "God is acting in all actions upon you. So respond to all actions upon you as to respond to his action."[16]

Niebuhr's clearest and most succinct discussion of the contextualism of ethics is found in his 1941 article "The Christian Church in the World's Crisis." Though directed to the specific problem of the church's ethical responsibility in the world, it exhibits the strong contextual character of his thought as well as reveals something of the way he relates religion and ethics.

Niebuhr begins his essay by setting out three propositions, the first two of which are directly relevant to the issue of contextualism:

(1) The religious issue in any particular time and place is less an issue about the specific content of actions than of the context in which each specific action is to be carried out.

(2) The important questions in the contemporary world crisis are religious questions about the context of political actions.[17]

These propositions contrast with two views Niebuhr finds unsatisfactory. On the one hand he rejects the view that "religious faith calls for specific sorts of domestic, economic, or political action, so that Christianity as such calls for the defense of democracy, or the adoption of socialism, or the policy of isolation, or conscientious objection to participation in war, or obedience to political authority, or marriage, or celibacy, or any one of a hundred similar specific actions." On the other hand, he finds the opposite extreme—"that since religious faith does not require specific political or other social actions, therefore it appears only in peculiarly religious actions"—equally unacceptable.[18] He rejects these two views because of the contextual character of all action:

> Actions are like words. Despite all efforts to discover the "real" meaning of a word by contemplating it long and thoughtfully, it reveals its meaning only in a sentence or paragraph in which the full intention of a speaker is made manifest. A single action apart from a total context may affect events, as an accident does, but not otherwise. It derives significance only from the context in which it stands; and the context which carries the action along, which makes it part of a total pattern, is determined by religion.[19]

Many of the perplexities in Niebuhr's ethical thought are clarified when viewed in this light. First, the lack of concrete moral judgments in his reflections is made perfectly intelligible: all actions have a context which is essentially determinative for their meaning. To ask for moral judgments on concrete ethical problems *in general* is to deny this and to think that a "dictionary" of moral judgments is possible. As Niebuhr makes clear in this article, the question of whether, for example, war is right or wrong cannot be answered abstractly, for much hinges on the context in which the decision for or against participation in war is made. His refusal to give pat answers to moral problems hence merely reflects his view that action takes on meaning only in an overarching context of interpretation and cannot be abstracted from such a context.

Second, Niebuhr's focus on the attitudes of those who act rather than on the act itself is made understandable by this context. One of the corollaries that Niebuhr draws from his propositions in "The Christian Church in the World's Crisis" is that "religious interest is directed more toward preceding and succeeding acts than toward the particular act of the moment."[20] The preceding acts are of interest because those acts are the internal motivations for the response, with the result that "the direction of the act . . . is determined by the direction of the actor rather than by its intrinsic nature."[21]

Finally, Niebuhr's strong individualistic emphasis is illuminated by his contextual analysis of action. Since the internal acts of the agent precedent to the action are more determinative than the intrinsic nature of the act, the only perspective able to take cognizance of those prior internal acts is the agent's own perspective. If indeed, motives are as central in ethical judgment as Niebuhr claims, only the individual agent will be able to make fully informed judgments concerning the motives from which that agent's own action springs.

In sum, Niebuhr's reluctance to make normative judgments on specific problems is due not to his disinterest in the practical relation of ethics to life but to the strong individualism and contextualism at the foundations of his thought. For Niebuhr, the ethicist's task is not to show what ethical decisions are right (for that is the prerogative of the individual who actually faces such decisions) but to elucidate the context, the patterns, and the structures involved in decision-making so that the individual can make more fully informed decisions.[22]

2. THE DEFINITION OF VALUE

Niebuhr's discussion of value also contains this character-istic reluctance to make normative judgments. One finds as little discussion of what specific things are abstractly good or bad as of what acts are abstractly right or wrong. Niebuhr's concern is more to illuminate the situation in which value occurs, to show its structures, its typical patterns, and its context than to develop a list of values that all persons, or even all Christians, should adopt. Hence his analysis of value is better judged by viewing it as an analysis of what the concept "value" means rather than a normative theory in which the central concern is to answer the question of what things are good.

The central claim around which Niebuhr builds his the-ory of value is that value is thoroughly relational in charac-ter. There is for Niebuhr no such thing as value in and of itself; value exists only in the context of relations between and among beings.[23] Value arises in, but is not reducible to, such relations. For "value is not a relation but arises in the relations of being to being."[24]

Niebuhr begins his essay "The Center of Value" by argu-ing not only that a relational understanding leads to a more adequate theory of value but also that such an understand-ing is implicit in those value theories which explicitly deny that value is relational. Niebuhr offers his relational theory not only as a metaethical proposal for understanding the meaning of value but also as a descriptive analysis of the way the idea of value is used by all value theorists. "What-ever may be the general reflections of value theorists on the meaning and nature of 'good,'" observes Niebuhr, "when they deal with more concrete ethical problems they usually employ a relational theory of value which defines good by reference to a being for which other beings are good."[25] Niebuhr notes that intuitionists and rationalists such as Plato, Nikolai Hartmann, and G. E. Moore, who tend to view value as an objective kind of being, and empiricists such as David Hume, who tend to view it subjectively, all revert to a relational position when it comes to the concrete definition of what is to be considered good. Niebuhr thus feels that his own analysis of value will illuminate even those theories that on first inspection appear diametrically opposed to his.

To say that value is a characteristic[26] of relations between and among beings is to say more than that value is exhaustively described when, between beings A and B, the relation AB is described as "good." Value is no more a characteristic of a relation in and of itself than it is of a being. Value is predicable of a being in a relation only with regard to some other being for whom that being is good. "Good" is predicable in the relation AB only insofar as A is good for B, or B is good for A, or the relation AB is good for some third being, C. The important point here is that whatever standpoint is taken, value can be said to be present only when the predication is made from that point of reference.

Because the predication of value necessarily involves some point of reference and is not merely predicable only of relations, Niebuhr's value theory is, I believe, *relativistic*. Distinguishing among three relational attributes will elucidate my point: the attributes of being yellow, being north of, and being pleasant. "Being yellow" is the most objective relational attribute of the three. The judgment "The car is yellow" is taken by most of us in our naive moments to refer to some quality objectively present in the car. But yellowness, as we come to learn in our first philosophy course, is not something adhering simply to the perceived object; it is a perceptual quality dependent on the relation between certain qualities of the surface of the object, certain qualities of the light striking the object, and certain qualities of the judging perceiver. Because human perceivers possess the same type of perceptual organs and have seen things that are called yellow, only as we carefully analyze the characteristics of yellowness can we see that it is a relational property and not an objective character of the object.

35

If two persons standing by the same car disagreed whether the car was yellow, and the disagreement was more than merely verbal (e.g., whether the yellow-green car was really more green than yellow or vice versa), most of us would think that something was terribly wrong. However, if the two disagreed over the judgment "The car is north of me," we would be troubled little at all, for "being north of" is a more obviously relational attribute. One of the two might well be on another side of the car. That the statement "The car is north" seems incomplete without a prepositional "of"-phrase further indicates how relational northness is.

Yet even in the case of "being north of," confirmation or disconfirmation of the judgment is possible, for there is an objective relation between the positions of the north pole, the car, and the one who says "The car is north of me." Another observer could confirm the relation among the three to be that the car is indeed north of the speaker. In this case, "The car is north of me" and "The car is north of that speaker" differ verbally but not substantively; both refer to the same relation among the car, the north pole, and the one who says "The car is north of me."

Our two observers could also disagree over the judgment "The car is pleasant." Yet here it is difficult to find objective points of reference by which to adjudicate the disagreement. Unlike "being north of," "being pleasant" involves a subjective relation, unknown to an observer unless the subject expresses an opinion on whether or not the car is pleasant. Such an opinion involves whether the subject presently finds, or has in the past found, the car pleasant.

Of these three relational attributes, Niebuhr's view of value corresponds most closely to "being north of." Value, like yellowness, "is objective in the sense that value relations are understood to be independent of the feelings of an observer but not in the sense that value is itself an objective kind of reality."[27] Unlike yellowness and like "being north of," however, the predication of value cannot be made unless the point of reference for the predication is specified. Then, however, the relations are objective, not dependent on the conscious feelings, valuations, interests, or perceptions of any observer.[28] The attribute "being pleasant" is too subjective, too dependent on the conscious feelings of a subject to be analogous to value. Pleasantness has no existence apart from consciously feeling subjects; value does. Value is present "wherever one existent being with capacities and potentialities confronts another existence that limits or completes or complements it."[29]

Niebuhr employs the idea of "need" to make clear that though value is always relative to some being, it does not depend on the conscious feelings, interests, or desires of that being. He contrasts "desires" with "needs":

A more adequate value-theory would . . . recognize . . . the relativity of values without prejudice to their objectivity. The interpretation of values as relative to structure and organic needs, rather than to desire and consciousness, provides for such an objective relativism.[30]

Relational value theory agrees with objectivism on this further point, that what is good-for-man, or for society or for any other being which represents the starting point of inquiry, is not determined by the desire of that being. Whether food or poison is good for animal existence has little to do with the desires in such existence; whether error or truth is good for the mind has little connection with the desire of an intellectual being for one or the other.[31]

"Need," of course, is often used in a subjective sense: I might say "I need a cigarette" when what I really mean is that I want or desire one. On the other hand, I might well say "I need to stop smoking," not necessarily meaning that I want to stop smoking but that smoking is not healthy. I am aware that there is an objective relation between health and smoking; smoking is bad for health whatever my own desires,

37

wants, or wishes. It is "need" in the second, objective sense that Niebuhr intends when he says that value is relative to need but not to desire.[32]

Value arises in two types of relational situations, according to Niebuhr. First of all, "value is present wherever one existent being with capacities and potentialities confronts another existence that limits or completes or complements it," that is, in the "reciprocity among existent beings." Second, value also occurs when "such existences are in a state of becoming, in which they are not yet what they 'ought' to be . . . in the sense that they have not yet achieved their own internal possibilities of becoming good for others."[33] Value is thus present in situations in which beings "fit" with each other as existent beings, as well as in situations in which beings are in the process of becoming themselves.

In his critique of Niebuhr's theory, George Schrader suggests

> that these two modes of value seem to be independent. Niebuhr seems to be saying that a being has value for itself as self-related *and* value for another and for itself because of its relation to other beings. The first premise involves a break in the relational structure of beings, a break which is seriously damaging to Niebuhr's general theory.[34]

Schrader's critique is directed at the earlier version of Niebuhr's essay, "The Center of Value,"[35] in which Niebuhr is less emphatic about the thoroughly social character of the relations that constitute value. For example, the second situation in which value appears is there described as "one in which existences are in a state of becoming, in which they are not yet what they 'ought' to be . . . in the sense that they have not yet achieved their own internal possibilities."[36] Comparing this sentence with its counterpart in the 1960 revision quoted above shows that Niebuhr has clarified the

38

meaning of "internal possibilities" by adding to it the phrase, "of becoming good for others."

In a footnote to the revised version Niebuhr acknowledges that his statement was "inadequate" in the earlier version but rejects Schrader's claim that seeing value in the situation of beings becoming what they ought to be involves a break in the relational structure of being:

> Since others also may encounter difficulties in understanding what I am trying to say I shall point out I do *not* wish to maintain that there is value in the self's relation to itself (or to its potential self) apart from its relation to others. The self's growth in intelligence, kindness, integrity, etc. is doubtless good or these are good, i.e., virtues; but their goodness is primarily their goodness for other selves; secondarily they are good-for-the-self as social being dependent not only on approval but on service of others. It is highly questionable for me whether we can call the virtues good in the self apart from their goodness for other selves or for the community of selves. The theory of value I am seeking to present is through and through social; I know of no self-relatedness apart from other-relatedness or self-alienation apart from alienation from the other. Potentiality in the whole realm of being is an important component in the situation in which there is value but the basis of this relational value theory is not the relation of existence to essence, it is that of self to other.[37]

Another way of expressing this view is to say that for Niebuhr all value is instrumental; a being is good only insofar as that being is good for some other being. No being is good simply in and of itself, not even in the sense that realization of potentialities is good apart from how such realization contributes to the good of others. No being is intrinsically good; hence no being, no thing, is intrinsically valuable.[38]

Since Niebuhr denies that any being is intrinsically valuable and since value is always relative to some being for whom something is said to be of value, Niebuhr's value theory may be termed a coherence theory of value. In a coherence theory of truth, a statement is judged to be true, not by its correspondence to some facts or states of affairs in the world, but by its coherence with and relation to other statements in a logical system. In this way the truth of each statement in the system depends on its relation to all other statements in the system. These other statements in turn depend on others in the system, so that no one statement in and of itself can be said to be true apart from its relations.

In the same way that the truth of a statement depends, in a coherence theory of truth, on its relation to other statements in a logical system, so does the value of a being depend, in Niebuhr's view, on its relation to other beings in a value system. One may take a being X as a point of reference, ask what is good for that being, and find that beings W, Y, and Z are good for X. But X itself is good only insofar as it is good for some other being V, and V is good only insofar as it is good for some other being U, etc. Moreover, U may itself be good for beings V, X, Y, and Z, with the result that any one value in the system presupposes the interdependence of many beings. "Thus relational value theory is concerned with a great multi-dimensionality of value, which is not the multi-dimensionality of an abstract realm of essential values but rather the multi-dimensionality of beings in their relations to each other." [39]

3. THE CENTER OF VALUE

The problem in everyday life is to choose among values that always compete and sometimes conflict. Niebuhr addresses the problem of normative value systems through his notion of the center of value. [40]

A value system is always relative to a being taken to be the center of value for that system. As we have seen, a being is good only insofar as it is good for some other being. Yet that other being is itself good only insofar as it is good for still some other being, and so on. One can never make a decision between conflicting values if the most one can do is follow out this never-ending regress of good-for-ness. Decision requires a point of reference in relation to which value judgments can be compared.

Niebuhr says that in the conflicts of value that impinge upon our action and our selves, we usually take some being as a center of value, as a point of reference for our decisions. In a value system which takes as its center of value humankind, for instance, all the singular judgments of value ultimately have to cohere with the judgment that what is good is good for humankind. Whether the smallpox virus is really good would, in such a human-centered system, ultimately rest on whether the smallpox virus were good for humankind. In a system which held as its center of value the evolutionary process, however, the question of the value of the smallpox virus might well be answered differently. For though it would no doubt still be the case that from the human standpoint the virus would not be good, from the definitive standpoint of the evolutionary process it might well be good in that it furthers the evolutionary process by impinging upon the survival of the human species, hence being one of the factors active in natural selection.

Value systems are therefore relative to some being taken for each system as the center of value. This is not to say, however, that such value centers are intrinsically valuable, for this would be to deny the thoroughly relational character of value.[41] Rather, in the chain of instrumental values, in that process of asking of each being in the value system what that being is good for, we reach some being about which the question is simply not asked. Our mind, our chain of questions, reaches a stopping point, some being beyond which we no longer find it necessary to ask, "Okay, but what is it good for?" Without such a relative stopping point, some center to which to refer our value judgments, value systems would be impossible. Hence "it is necessary to take one's standpoint with or in some being accepted as *the center of value* if one is to construct anything like a consistent system of value judgments and determinations of what is right."[42]

The relativity of all centers of value means, on the one hand, that all value systems are "dogmatically relativistic." A consistent system of value could indeed conceivably be formed around each and every being if each were taken as a center of value. Niebuhr argues that

> there can be as many theoretical value systems as there are beings in existence. Yet none of these relative systems is relativistic in the sense of being dependent on feeling or desire; each can be objective in the sense that it may be a system dealing with actual value relations and in the sense that the value judgments made within that frame of reference are subject to critical inquiry into their truth or falsity.[43]

On the other hand, the relativity of those centers means that the adoption of such a center is religious in character, because "every such theory adopts as its explicit or implicit starting point some being or beings in relation to which good is judged to be good and evil evil, in relation to which also the rightness or wrongness of its relations to other beings is examined."[44] These centers of value, these "dogmas of ethics," are "assertions of faith, confessions of trust in something which makes life worth living, commitments of the self to a god."[45] Niebuhr's value theory thus leads ineluctably to his concept of God.

CHAPTER FOUR

God in Niebuhr's
Discussion of Value

IN NIEBUHR'S THEORY of value, "God" functions in several different roles. But a discussion of these roles depends on the close relationship between value systems and faith in Niebuhr's thought.

1. THE NATURE OF FAITH

Niebuhr's discussion of faith is but the existential and practical side of many of the ideas he develops at the theoretical level in his analysis of value. This is not to say that for Niebuhr faith and valuation are identical human activities. He is careful to maintain that the reduction of faith to human valuation is a distortion of it.[1] Nevertheless, his analysis of faith and his value theory are very closely interdependent.

This interdependence is especially evident in his *Radical Monotheism and Western Culture*. In that work he attempts to view faith as a generic human phenomenon, part of our common life as selves. He wants "to describe a fundamental personal attitude which, whether we call it *faith* or give it some other name, is apparently universal or general enough to be widely recognized." Note the extensive use of value language as Niebuhr specifies what he means by faith:

This is the attitude and action of confidence in, and fidelity to, certain realities as the sources of value and the objects of loyalty. This personal attitude or action is am-

43

bivalent; it involves reference to the value that attaches to the self and to the value toward which the self is directed. On the one hand it is trust in that which gives value to the self; on the other it is loyalty to what the self values.[2]

The dynamics of faith here involve two moments—trust and loyalty—each of which is defined by reference to value. Trust is the component of faith that correlates with the self's sense that it is valued. That which is a source or center of value is experienced in this mode as that which values the self, and existentially this mode is prior to loyalty.[3] On this source or center of value the self "depends not only for his own meaning but for the worth of everything else he encounters."[4]

As the response of trust is elicited by the self's realization that it derives its value from some being which is its source of value, so the response of loyalty is elicited by the recognition of the value that attaches to the source itself. As "faith-trust" elicits a confession of faith in the value-center, "faith-loyalty" elicits a vow of commitment to that value-center. It is the active side of faith, whereas trust is the passive.[5]

To have faith in a being is to sense that one is valued by that being and to value that being in turn; it is to trust and be loyal to that being. But on what is that trust and loyalty based? According to Niebuhr, it is based on some third being to whom both other beings are mutually faithful. Niebuhr uses the following example to illustrate the triadic character of faith:

> Think of two soldiers in Korea in the late war. They are bound together by loyalty to each other. And they trust in each other's loyalty, that they will not let each other down. This seems to be the central feature of their existence. They are not going to desert, because they are not going to let their companions down. They are not

44

going to desert because they believe their companions
will not let them down. And all the fears are overcome
or quenched in some way in the act of mutual loyalty.
But then there is something else there. They are in this
situation as those who are required to be and who are
loyal to a cause that includes both of them and that concerns both of them. They call it the United States, perhaps, or they call it democracy, or civilization. Now
their loyalty to the cause may be a less tangible or less
real thing than their loyalty to each other but nevertheless the cause is there. It has put them together, at that
point, and they believe somehow, that the other fellow
will not be disloyal to the common cause. Then they
have to believe a third thing of which the soldiers are
very often dubious. Namely, that the common cause
will not be disloyal to them. That it will not deceive
them. Here in this patriotic situation a structure of confidence, trust, and loyalty begins to appear which looks
something like this. I trust the companion in his loyalty
to me, and in his loyalty to the cause to which I am also
trying to be faithful. I expect his trust in me as one who
will not only never let him down but as one who will not
let down the cause and then I somehow try to trust the
cause, that which transcends us both as that which will
not let him down or deceive him and which will not deceive me or let me down. Here is at least a kind of triad
of faith.[6]

Niebuhr acknowledges how closely this analysis of faith-
loyalty follows that of Josiah Royce in *The Philosophy of Loyalty*. Niebuhr, however, departs from Royce at the point
where Royce suggests that the third entity to which loyal
selves are mutually loyal is the principle of loyalty itself.[7]
Niebuhr argues that the triadic structure of loyalty is always
a structure that relates three *beings*. As is the case with value,
loyalty or faith is not some being but a relation among beings. Hence we cannot "identify the transcendent object of

loyalty, as Royce does, with loyalty itself, since loyalty relates one to a cause and in any form in which it is conceivable points beyond itself to something that transcends it."[8]

The similarity between Niebuhr's analysis of faith and his analysis of value can now more clearly be seen. First of all, both have a triadic structure wherein the relation between two entities is determined by some third thing. The value of being A for being B finally rests, in a value system, on how B as well as A are good for some third being C taken as a center of value. The loyalty of self A to self B itself depends on the way that A and B are themselves loyal to some third being which Niebuhr calls the "cause" or the "center of value."[9]

Second, that Niebuhr uses the same term "center of value" to refer to the third being involved in both structures itself indicates the close relationship between faith and value in his thought. Their difference is similar to the difference between internal and external history that Niebuhr develops in *The Meaning of Revelation*. He talks about centers of value from two different perspectives, one impersonal and objective, the other personal and subjective.[10] In his value theory he speaks of centers of value from a theoretical, objective point of view. He wants to unfold the way that value judgments are made and the way that selves think about value. When he talks about value centers from the perspective of faith, however, he approaches them from a more existential, subjective perspective. He analyzes not how *judgments* are made but how *selves* have faith that enables them to live in the world. In his value theory a center of value is defined as the being that serves as the standpoint in relation to which good-for-ness is finally defined; the determination of such a center is necessary for constructing "a consistent system of value judgments and determinations of what is right."[11] In his discussion of faith, however, the value centers are most often described as the beings which are "able to bestow significance and worth on our existence"[12] or which make "life worth living." [13] Such centers are necessary since "we cannot live without a cause, without some object of devotion, some center of worth, something on which we rely for our meaning." [14] Unless Niebuhr uses "value centers" and "centers of value" equivocally, two different perspectives must be at stake, one objective and one subjective, on what appears to be the same idea.

2. HENOTHEISM AND POLYTHEISM

In analyzing Niebuhr's thought it has been difficult to delay until now examination of the idea of God. Both Niebuhr's value theory and his understanding of faith unfold toward that idea and seem truncated without it. However, both his value theory and his understanding of faith are developed as phenomenological and philosophical proposals about generic human structures of experience and explicitly avoid dogmatically theological appeals to positive Christian doctrines. When he introduces the idea of God in his discussion of value he does not merely overlay his philosophical and phenomenological analysis with a concept derived from Christian dogmatics.

Of course, the idea of God is implicit from the outset in his analyses of value theory and of faith. Niebuhr did not start out as a value theorist and then become a theologian. Nevertheless he intends to make a case for his view of God in such a way that the *logic* of introducing the idea in his discussion is based on the inner necessity of his argument rather than extraneous factors.

At the most general level, Niebuhr simply uses "god" as another word for what he means by "center of value" or "value center." As such, it is a formal designation, functionally defined, whose material content, as we shall see, can vary. Since it is a concept synonymous to "value center," and since we have already examined that latter concept's function in both Niebuhr's theory of value and his understanding of

47

faith, we need now only show that "god" and "center of value" are at least in some uses, for Niebuhr, truly synonyms.

That task is complicated by the very grammar of the word "God" in ordinary language. "God" functions in our language as both a common noun and a personal name; these two functions can be seen in our use of "god" without capitalization yet with an article, and in our use of "God" capitalized without an article. In the former sense we can speak of "the gods of Greece," or "a god of the Roman pantheon," or even "the god of Christianity." In these uses "god" simply refers to a type of being with certain characteristics, just as "chair" refers to a type of object with certain characteristics. In its other use, however, "God" functions as the personal name of a unique individual, analogous to the way that "Yahweh" is the name of the Hebrew god in the Old Testament. In everyday language we use the term both ways.

Niebuhr does too, and that makes showing the synonymity of "god" and "center of value" in his thought more difficult. When Niebuhr speaks of "gods" in the common sense, he uses the term as a synonym for "center of value." This is clear in his article "Faith in Gods and in God" (whose title itself employs both senses of "god" as common noun and as name). He begins that article with an analysis of the phenomenon of human faith and argues that "without such . . . faith we do not and cannot live." This faith, which ultimately boils down to the faith that "life is worth living, or better, [this] reliance on certain centers of value as able to bestow significance and worth on our existence," implicitly impels us on toward the concept of a god, since "to have faith and to have a god is one and the same thing." Hence "the word 'god' means the object of human faith in life's worthwhileness." [15]

An even more explicit identification of "gods" with "centers of value" can be found in *Radical Monotheism and Western Culture*. In the following passage from that work "gods" is used as a common noun, indicated by the use of the lower case:

In ordinary discourse the word "gods" has many meanings. Now we mean by it the powers on which men call for help in time of trouble; now the forces which they summon up in their search for ecstasy; now the realities before which they experience awe and the sense of the holy; now the beings they posit in their speculative efforts to explain the origin and government of things; now the objects of adoration. The question whether religion in which all these attitudes and activities are present is a single movement of the mind and with it the query whether the word "gods" refers to entities of one class must be left to other contexts. We are concerned now with faith as dependence on a value-center and as loyalty to a cause. Hence when we speak of "gods" we mean the gods of faith, namely, such value-centers and causes.[16]

The explicit identification of "gods" and "value-centers" in *Radical Monotheism and Western Culture* makes it all the more interesting that Niebuhr does not so explicitly equate them in his essay "The Center of Value." He comes close to making the identification in this essay, calling philosophical theories which posit two or more value centers "polytheistic" and talking of values being "deified" as the value center.[17] Yet he never openly identifies "gods" with "centers of value."

Reasons why he does not can be adduced. First of all, this piece is directed to a philosophical audience in an attempt to develop a theory of value conversant with other theories. For this purpose it is sufficient to use "centers of value" without also employing the term "gods" as an alternative. Further, such use avoids confusing the issue at stake—the relational and relative character of value—by the use of a term that would immediately raise a red flag for many philosophically inclined readers. Finally, this essay is one in which Niebuhr uses "God" only in its sense as a proper name. The term does occur, but not in reference to any cen-

49

ter of value; rather "God" names a specific center, that of radically monotheistic faith.

Niebuhr does not leave his analysis of the idea of god at this formal and general level. He begins to fill out the formal definition of a god as a value center in his analysis of the differing forms of human faith as henotheism, polytheism, and radical monotheism. These categories show how thoroughly interdependent are his understandings of value, faith, and god.

Since "atheism seems as irreconcilable with human existence as is radical skepticism in the actuality of the things we eat, and breathe, walk upon and bump into,"[18] the issue based on which Niebuhr develops his typology of faiths is not whether there is a god but rather the character of the gods in whom humans believe; or as he puts it in an early article, "the important question for religion is not the question, whether a god exists, but rather, what being or beings have the value of deity."[19] In order to explore the different sorts of gods that serve as objects of faith, Niebuhr characterizes three types of human faith.

The distinctions among these types of faith logically rest on four possible combinations of two sets of polar alternatives: One-many and finite-infinite. However, Niebuhr uses only three of these four combinations. One of them—the gods as infinite and many—is logically inconceivable.[20] The three remaining characterizations—the gods as finite and many, a god as finite and one, and the god as infinite and one—correspond, respectively, to the human faiths of polytheism, henotheism, and radical monotheism. (See figure 1.)

Polytheism in human faith occurs where there are multiple value centers to which trust and loyalty are given. Because these multiple centers are not themselves comprehended by some more inclusive center of value, a pluralism of value centers remains. The self in its attempt to have faith is forced to have many faiths—now in this value center, now in another—and no unification is possible because there is no unity among the self's gods.

FIGURE 1

INFINITE

	infinite and one	infinite and many	
	"radical monotheism"	(logically inconceivable)	
O N E			M A N Y
	finite and one	finite and many	
	"henotheism"	"polytheism"	

FINITE

Niebuhr accuses many philosophical value theories of being polytheistic in that they rest on multiple value systems, each with a different center of value, "confine themselves to two or three of these relative systems, and then become involved in questions about their interrelations."[21] As an example he examines the value theories of Nikolai Hartmann and of utilitarianism and concludes:

So on the one hand Hartmann presents us with a kind of Epicurean faith in which the center of value is the realm of ideal essences which have their being above the world of existences in self-sufficiency, yet so that only in relation to them anything else has value. On the other hand man is his center of value, in relation to whom even the ideas of value alone have actual worth. Or [in the case of utilitarianism] the polytheism is that of human society and the human individual and the community of living beings as centers of value which must somehow be reconciled.[22]

But for Niebuhr such reconciliation cannot take place unless one moves beyond polytheism to henotheism or radical monotheism.

Unlike polytheism, henotheism holds only one god to be its center of value; yet that god is one finite reality among others. One being amidst the great multidimensionality of value is elevated to a position of pre-eminence as that single source from which value derives and that single cause to which loyalty is owed. The conflict within the self, characteristic of the polytheist, that arises from having to decide among multiple value centers dissipates within henotheism. Yet that conflict does not disappear; it merely moves to the social level. Since different finite realities can function for different selves as their gods, conflict between and among selves over their gods becomes inevitable.

Niebuhr also calls henotheism "social faith" because some social reality is usually taken to be god. He cites nationalism as an example. Nationalistic henotheists adopt as their center of value the community of the state with its aims and goals:

Every participant in the group derives his value from his position in the enduring life of the community. Here he is related to an actuality that transcends his own, that continues to be though he ceases to exist. He is dependent on it as it is not dependent on him. And this applies even more to his significance than to his existence. The community is not so much his great good as the source and center of all that is good, including his own value. But the society is also his cause; its continuation, power, and glory are the unifying end of all his actions. The standard by which he judges himself and his deeds, his companions and their actions, by which also he knows himself to be judged, is the standard of loyalty to the community.[23]

Niebuhr cites other examples of henotheistic human faiths: a naturalism which sees nature as the ultimate value center, a humanism which sees humankind as the being in reference to which value judgments are made and to which our ultimate loyalty is owed, and a vitalism which sees living things and the principle of life standing behind those living things as its god. All these forms of henotheism elevate some finite being to the place of the singular value center or god.

3. RADICAL MONOTHEISM'S GOD

Henotheism and polytheism for Niebuhr fail as adequate forms of human faith, and henotheistic and polytheistic gods fail to serve as adequate centers of value. If we are polytheists, "we are divided within ourselves and socially by our religion."[24] We honor now this god, now some other, without any unifying center by which to bring together the confusing din of values. "The best we can achieve in this realm is a sort of compromise among many absolute claims . . . with many faiths held in succession"; it is "a kind of successive polygamy, being married now to this and now to that object of devotion."[25] Niebuhr finds, however, such a compromise unsatisfactory because we experience our self as *a* self. The experience of such a unitary self demands as its counterpart a unitary God.[26] Polytheism therefore cannot make intelligible the basic experience of self that stands behind all our attempts to interpret our experience in the world.[27]

Henotheism, too, fails to satisfy the human need for faith. Henotheists recognize the need for a single center of value, for a single god to bring intelligibility to the experience of the self's unity. But they put their faith in a god who, as a finite being, cannot "guarantee meaning to our life in the

53

world save for a time."[28] Nor can such a finite god demand
loyalty universally enough to be the one god of all being. As
a result, henotheistic gods not only cannot guarantee meaning to our life, they show themselves to be false gods, so that
"at the end nothing is left to defend us against the void of
meaninglessness."[29] What is needed instead is a god that is
singular and infinite. And Niebuhr finds such a god in the
God of radical monotheism.[30]

Niebuhr employs a variety of metaphors to discuss the Infinite One of radical monotheism. However, three types of
metaphors predominate—the Infinite as the transcendent
Absolute, as the encompassing Universal, and as the principle of Being.

The metaphor of the transcendent Absolute sharply distinguishes God from all finite being. The Absolute is con-
trasted with the relative; Absolute Being is distinguished
from all relative being. Niebuhr typically employs this type
of metaphor when the radically monotheistic God functions
in his thought as a relativizing principle to human judgments, institutions, and beliefs that are taken in themselves
to be absolute. It reminds us "that none is absolute save God
and that the absolutizing of anything finite is ruinous to the
finite itself."[31]

The metaphor of God as transcendent Absolute plays a
crucial role in Niebuhr's theory of value and is the principle
image around which his analysis pivots in "The Center of
Value." Niebuhr concludes that article by indicating how
monotheistic faith relates to his theory of value. His conclusion rests on his premise that each value judgment is relative to some being taken to be, for that judgment, the center
of value. Yet such a value center is not itself intrinsically
valuable (for that would deny the relational character of all
value) but is simply that being beyond which the question of
what it is good for is no longer asked. For monotheistic faith
the value center is "the transcendent One for whom alone
there is an ultimate good and for whom, as the source and
end of all things, whatever is, is good." Yet instead of func-

tioning as a center of value which positively informs the monotheist's value system, God in this article plays more the role of a critical principle, relativizing all the finite value systems that we as human beings variously employ. In the following passage Niebuhr distinguishes between monotheistic value theory and relative value systems:

> With this beginning the value theory of monotheistic theology is enabled to proceed to the construction of many relative value systems, each of them tentative, experimental, and objective, as it considers the interaction of beings on beings, now from the point of view of man, now from the point of view of society, now from the point of view of life. But it is restrained from erecting any one of these into an absolute, or even from ordering it above the others, as when the human-centered value system is regarded as superior to a life-centered system. A monotheistically centered value theory is not only compatible with such objective relativism in value analysis but requires it in view of its fundamental dogma that none is absolute save God and that the absolutizing of anything finite is ruinous to the finite itself.[32]

Radical monotheism's center of value does not function here as a center for a monotheistic value system. If its God were to become such a center, then it would be one center among other possible centers in the great multidimensionality of being; as a result, the Infinite Absolute would be brought down to the level of finite being, and radical monotheism would become merely another form of henotheism. To preserve the transcendence of the One beyond the many, Niebuhr suggests a unique function for radical monotheism's center of value. Instead of being the point of reference for actual judgments within a value system, it becomes a critical principle relativizing all actual, concrete value systems and the decisions made in them. The center serves to remind us in our actual use of finite value systems that these are relative systems, so that we are "restrained from erecting any one of these into an absolute, or even from ordering it above the others." The result is a kind of democracy of finite value centers: all are equally close to and at the same time far from the transcendent Center of Value for whom whatever is, is good.

The second type of metaphor that Niebuhr employs is God as the encompassing Universal. Instead of distinguishing the infinite as over against the finite, this image places the finite within the infinite, the many within the One. "I believe," says Niebuhr, using this type of metaphor, "that man exists and moves and has his being in God."[33]

Under this metaphor, Niebuhr at points identifies God with the whole of being in such a way that a strain of pantheistic imagery can be discerned. Yet he never simply identifies God with the totality of the world. Even when he does identify God with Being, he immediately suggests that his intention is better expressed by such phrases as "the principle of being," "the source of all things," and "the power by which they exist."[34] Yet as Paul Tillich rightly observes,

> pantheism does not mean, never has meant, and never should mean that everything that is, is God. . . . Pantheism is the doctrine that God is the substance or essence of all things, not the meaningless assertion that God is the totality of things.[35]

In this more refined sense, pantheistic tendencies are evident in Niebuhr's work and show up when he uses this type of metaphor for God.

These tendencies can be seen in Niebuhr's article on the Christian response to the Japanese invasion of Manchuria, "The Grace of Doing Nothing."[36] This article, because of its suggestion of moral quietism, drew a sharp response from Niebuhr's brother, Reinhold. Reinhold accused him of an unrealistic ethical perfectionism. "Love," says Reinhold, may qualify the social struggle of history but it will never abolish it, and those who make the attempt to bring society under the dominion of love will die on the cross. And those who behold the cross are quite right in seeing it as a revelation of the divine, of what man ought to be but cannot be, at least so long as he is en-meshed in the process of history.[37]

H. Richard responded to that article with another, "A Communication: The Only Way into the Kingdom of God." Here pantheistic tendencies are clearly evidenced:

For my brother God is outside the historical processes, so much that he charges me with faith in a miracle-working deity which interferes occasionally, sometimes brutally, sometimes redemptively, in this history. But God, I believe, is always in history; *he is the structure in things*, the source of all meaning, the "I am that I am," that which is that it is.[38]

Niebuhr also expresses this view of God as Universal Being in his 1943 contribution to a seminar at the University of Michigan on the nature and existence of God, published later that year by *Motive* magazine.[39] Note the dark strokes with which Niebuhr characterizes the infinite reality that monotheists learn to call their God:

We may call it the nature of things, we may call it fate, we may call it reality. But by whatever name we call it, this law of things, this reality, this way things are, is something with which we all must reckon. We may not be able to give a name to it, calling it only the "void" out of which everything comes and to which everything returns, though that is also a name. But it is there—the last shadowy and vague reality, the secret of existence by virtue of which things come into being, are what they are, and pass away. Against it there is no defense.

This reality, this nature of things, abides when all else passes. It is the source of all things and the end of all. It surrounds our life as the great abyss into which all things plunge and as the great source whence they all come. What it is we do not know save that it is and that it is the supreme reality with which we reckon.[40]

When universal Being instead of the transcendent Absolute is used to characterize the value center, a different relationship comes into play between the center and all actual value systems. If the whole of being is the value center, then all is included within the center. As a result, all being is seen as good, not because it is good for the value center, but because it is the value center. Every being, as a member of being, participates in the center so that Niebuhr is able to say, in Augustinian fashion, "whatever is, is good." All the relative value systems with their relative centers are superseded by the all-inclusive center and the corresponding all-inclusive value system.

There are problems with this way of speaking of the monotheist's center of value. On the one hand, if the whole of reality is the center of value, then "center" loses all possible meaning. "Center" implies a corresponding circumference, something that is not the center. But if all of being is seen as a center, then what could the center be a center of? On the other hand, this way of speaking is inconsistent with the relational character of value that lies at the roots of Niebuhr's theory. Things can be said to be good only insofar as they are good for something else; we reach our center of value when we reach some being about which we no longer ask what it is good for, though it too must logically be good for something else if all value is relational. But if universal Being is taken as the center of value, it becomes logically impossible for universal Being to be good for anything else since as universal Being it must include all being within itself.

It could be argued that universal Being is good for the

beings it comprises, as a whole is good for its parts, and that therefore value is present in the relation of the whole to its parts. However, such an argument is inconsistent with Niebuhr's thoroughly relational view of value because it depends on the idea of internal relations. Niebuhr, it will be remembered, denies that internal relations within a being are sufficient conditions for the presence of value; he rejects the attribution of value in a situation in which a being's existence is related to its own essence.[41] Therefore, he would certainly not be satisfied with using the internal relations within universal Being as a way of dealing with the value of universal Being.

Because he recognizes these problems, Niebuhr adopts a third type of metaphor for speaking about the monotheist's god, the metaphor of the Infinite One as the principle of being. This way of conceiving God enables him to preserve the universality of the goodness of being, and yet avoid, to a degree, the problems that attach to identifying the center of value with universal being. This metaphor is based on the triadic structure of loyalty and is heavily influenced by the thought of Paul Tillich.[42]

The metaphor of the Infinite One as the principle of being—also found in such formulations as "the source of all things," "the beginner and perfector of all there is," "the mystery of being beyond being," "the Fountain of being," and "the ground of all being"—combines the advantages of the previous metaphors. Characteristic of its formulations is that God is seen as intimately related to, yet carefully distinguished from, the realm of being. As the principle or ground of being, God is compresent in all being, yet present in such a way that, with Tillich, Niebuhr can affirm that "God is beyond being."[43] In Niebuhr's theory of responsibility this is expressed in the interpretation that all action upon us is in fact God's action.[44] The totality of our conditions is our confrontation with God; yet we confront God's actions not God's self (which is what we are up against according to the metaphor of God as universal Being). God stands behind the reality of being and yet is agentially responsible for that being in a direct and immediate way.

Distinguishing God from the realm of being in such a way that God remains intimately related to that realm enables Niebuhr to employ the triadic character of loyalty to relate the three primary entities in his analysis of God as the principle of being—the self, the realm of being, and God. Niebuhr, as we have seen, employs Royce's triadic analysis of loyalty in his analysis of faith: the relation between two selves always involves a reference to a third entity. "When we reflect about this third reality that is present to us in all our responses to our companions," says Niebuhr, "we note that it has a double character. On the one hand it is something personal; on the other it contains within itself again a reference to something that transcends it or to which it refers." Two patriots, for example, may be loyal to each other for the sake of their country. Yet the country contains an implicit reference to a cause beyond itself, which in turn relates the patriots in loyalty to the country. Niebuhr uses democracy as an example of such a cause. But democracy implicitly refers to a third reality that unites the self with it, so that "ultimately we arrive in the case of democracy at a community which refers beyond itself to humanity and which in doing so seems to envisage not only representatives of the human community as such but a universal society and a universal generalized other, Nature and Nature's God." Hence, "the process of self-transcendence or of reference to the third beyond each third does not come to rest until the total community of being has been involved."[45] At this point

there appears on the horizon of our inquiry the mystery of the Transcendent. It seems that when we deal with the structures of faith as we find them in our ordinary experience we are dealing with realities that point beyond themselves to a cause beyond all causes, to an object of loyalty beyond all concrete persons and abstract values, to the Being or Ground of Being which obliges and demands trust, which unites us in a universal community. . . . Behind the faiths and communities of faith in which we are united in family and nation and company of scholars there looms the grand structure of a community of faith which is universal, in which all selves are involved as companions and in which the third, the cause and the object of trust, is the Transcendent reality, present wherever two or three are present to each other or anyone is present to himself.[46]

At that transcendent ground of being that serves as the cause of the universal community of being, does the triadic structure of loyalty reach an impasse? Is there a cause that unites the self with God, or can we no longer seek a third beyond the self and God which unites these two in common loyalty? Here Niebuhr makes an interesting move. Rather than halting the triadic analysis, he makes the cause which stands behind the loyalty of self and God reflexive. God's cause is the universal community of being just as that universal community's cause is God. Rather than standing above the relation of God and self, God's cause stands below it. As a result, the radical monotheist's

cause also has a certain duality. On the one hand it is the principle of being itself; on the other, it is the realm of being. Whether to emphasize the one or the other may be unimportant, since the principle of being has a cause, namely, the realm of being, so that loyalty to the principle of being must include loyalty to its cause; loyalty to the realm of being, on the other hand, implies keeping faith with the principle by virtue of which it is, and is one realm.[47]

The other aspect of the double character of the third reality is that it is something personal.[48] Thus as the cause behind the universal community, the principle of being must itself be personal: "the cornerstone of . . . all radical monotheist confidence and loyalty is that the one God who is Being is an 'I,' or like an 'I,' who is faithful as only selves are faithful."[49] Faith is an interpersonal relation among selves. When we talk of trust and loyalty we must speak in personal and not impersonal terms, for the personal is the proper home of such speech.

Niebuhr's analysis of the ever-more inclusive triads of trust and loyalty involves at each step along the way a reference to a community of persons. When he speaks of patriots related to each other by the cause that is their country, he speaks of the country as in part being constituted by "a community of persons living and dead—heroes of the past and future, founding fathers and historical posterity." The country is in turn constituted by a cause which stands behind the relation between the patriot and that "community of persons living and dead," that cause being democracy in the case of America. But then democracy is itself constituted in part by a "transcendent reference group" of persons, and the patriot relates to democracy by relating to that group of persons. This reference to a third, implying a reference to still another third continues:

> But now the transcendent reference group—these founding fathers, for instance, encountered in memory and these representatives of the community in a later time encountered in anticipation—refer beyond themselves. They are persons who stand for something and represent something. They represent not the community only but what the community stands for. Ultimately we arrive in the case of democracy at a community which refers beyond itself to humanity and which in doing so seems to envisage not only representatives of the human community as such but a universal society and a universal generalized other, Nature and Nature's God.[50]

This analysis of the ever-expanding communities of trust and loyalty depends on the presence of a transcendent reference group of persons at each step along the way. Such reference groups can indeed be envisioned up to the level of humanity because to that point the ever-more inclusive communities are communities of persons. But this becomes more difficult as the communites expand beyond humanity. What transcendent reference group of persons would be involved in the cause of living things, or of nature, or of being in general? It is hard to see how Niebuhr would at these levels follow out his triadic analysis, resting as it does on a reference to a community of persons. It is difficult, therefore, to arrive at a universal community by the kind of analysis that Niebuhr seems to suggest, because the community at which his analysis finally aims is not a community of persons. And that line of analysis would be necessary for Niebuhr's discussion to get where he wants to go from where he starts.[51]

What really lies behind Niebuhr's analysis is the Christian vision of a universal community of being under a transcendent reference person, that is, the Kingdom of God. Given this starting point, the cause of the totality of being is appropriately conceived as something personal. But the argument he develops using the triadic character of trust and loyalty will not arrive at that point on its own. One can get to the universal community of being only by beginning with the Universal Person.

4. GOD AND CONCRETE VALUE JUDGMENTS

Thus, the metaphor of God as the transcendent Absolute functions as a critical relativizing principle, equalizing all finite value systems before the Absolute for whom whatever is, is good. This critical principle does not interact positively with those finite systems nor does it provide a standard by which comparatively to rank values within those systems. Further, the metaphor of God as the encompassing Universal functions differently. By including all being within its value center it too equalizes all finite values; but rather than doing so by making all finite being equally distant from the Absolute, it does so by making whatever is, good by virtue of its participation in the center. Its function with respect to concrete value judgments is primarily valuational: conceiving God in this way makes the whole of being good.

The metaphor of God as the principle of being retains this valuational character, yet does so in a way that does not collapse the triadic structure of Niebuhr's analysis of value—a collapse characteristic of conceiving God as the encompassing Universal. By maintaining the distinctiveness of self, the realm of being, and God, Niebuhr is able by this third metaphor to hold that the universal realm of being is good because it is good for God, because it is good in reference to the center of value of radical monotheism. At the same time, this metaphor also incorporates to a degree the relativizing function that we saw operative in the metaphor of God as transcendent Absolute, in that it also significantly distinguishes finite beings' value for God from their value for each other. Because the metaphor of God as principle of being incorporates the functions of the other two metaphors, it is not surprising to find it predominating over the others in Niebuhr's corpus.

The two functions of the monotheistic God can be seen in Niebuhr's discussion of the radical monotheism undergirding science. On the one hand:

> Something like the radical faith in the principle of being as center of value and in the realm of being as cause, seems to the theologian to be present first of all in a negative form in the established habit of scientific skepticism toward all claims to absolute significance on the part of any finite being and of the absolute truth of any theory of being. In the endeavor of science to rid itself of all anthropomorphism and anthropocentrism, of all tendencies to regard man as the measure of all

64

things, whether of their nature or of their value, he notes the presence of movement like that of radical faith in religion. . . . In this negative movement of scientific skepticism something is present which is like that *via negativa* in the religion which denies the name of God to any limited form or power, not because it doubts the reality of the One beyond the many but because it believes in him.

On the other:

More positively radical faith in that One seems present to the theological point of view in the confidence with which pure science seems to approach anything and everything in the world as potentially meaningful. . . . Whatever is, in the world of being and becoming, is worthy of inquiry not because of its intrinsic worth nor yet because it is part of some familiar pattern of meanings, but because it *is*, because in its existence it participates in being and is related to the universal and the unitary.[52]

At the concrete level of actual value decisions neither of these functions of the monotheistic God provides much direction as to the value relation to choose in the face of competing value claims. In its relativizing function the radically monotheistic idea of God implies about a conflict of values: No value is absolute and all values are relatively insignificant in the face of the Absolute Valuer. This does not provide any concrete standard for comparing relative values with each other. In its valuational function the idea suggests such a standard in its claim that for the God of radical monotheism, whatever is, is good. But the universal valuation of all being as good fails to provide a criterion by which beings can be comparatively judged. If every being is good for God and none can be said to be better for God than others, then there is no basis for comparative judgments. As far as our value decisions go, it is as if nothing were good for God; all our relative goods are relative nonetheless. If Niebuhr could speak of comparative degrees of being, he could maintain that whatever is, is good and yet still have grounds to make comparative judgments of value; they would then correlate with the differing degrees of being. Yet Niebuhr consistently refuses to employ this Neoplatonic solution to the problem.[53]

Niebuhr at times hints of a more positive relation between the absolute value relation in which everything is good for God and concrete decisions among relative values. But he never directly connects these hints to the problem of comparative value. He suggests in his "Concluding Unscientific Postscript" to *Christ and Culture* that when we "deal as we must with the relative values of persons, things, and movements" we must "remember that all these realities which have many values in relation to each other also have a relation to God that must never be lost to view." This makes "room not only for relative justice but for the formation and reformation of relative judgments by reference to the absolute relation." He then gives an example:

> The relation to the Absolute will not come into consideration as an afterthought—as when a priest is sent to accompany a criminal on the way to the gallows—but as a forethought and a cothought that determines how everything is done that is done to him and for him. Provisions for fair trial, for the checking and balancing of partial, relative judgments, for the prohibition of certain kinds of punishment, for the physical, spiritual care of the offender, for his restoration to society— these may all reflect recognition of his value beyond all relative values.

The criminal's value for God, however, cannot be made the sole criterion of value. "If I consider," says Niebuhr, "only the value my neighbor has to God and ignore his value for

66

other men . . . I am not acting with piety but with impiety, for I am not exercising any faith in the actual God who has created neither me nor my neighbor as only-begotten sons but as brothers."[54] Rather, the absolute value relation of all being to God provides a background, a context in which to make decisions among relative values. It may indeed shape those decisions; it may even "formulate and reformulate" the way that those decisions are made. But it will not make those relative decisions in any way absolute. In spite of the recognition that the criminal is good for God, we still judge the criminal to be criminal, to be bad for society, because the decisive criteria that we appeal to are the criteria of our relative value systems. For Niebuhr this is not so much a failing to be overcome as it is a part of the structure of reality to be accepted.

In his Christian ethics lectures Niebuhr examined the relation between relative values and absolute values under the rubric of his discussion of the response to God as Creator. The doctrine that God created the creation as good means that believers must recognize "the great equalitarianism in the world of creation [and] respond to whatever is, appreciatively, affirmatively. To respond to God in all responses to things is to affirm the world, life, being." Yet Niebuhr recognizes that "within this world affirmation choices must be made. All things [are] loveworthy as his creations, but we cannot equally love, equally cultivate all beings since we are finite."

Niebuhr outlines several methods used in history to make choices among values. He finds, for example, a spiritualistic scale at work in Christian history: God is spirit, therefore "spiritual beings are nearer to him than material." A humanistic scale has also been used in which humankind has been viewed as closest to God and therefore higher in value. But Niebuhr finds something arbitrary in these scales, something that fails to take seriously that the whole of being is God's creation, that whatever is, is good. Niebuhr even finds the value scale based on inclusiveness, in which "that is a higher value which is more inclusive," has limitations—a fact all the more interesting in the context of Niebuhr's attraction to universality as an important component in the analysis of radically monotheistic faith. Indeed, he finds no satisfactory scale to span the gap between the Absolute value relation of all being to God and the relative value relations that persons use to make concrete decisions.

Realizing the eminent practical need for criteria to aid decision, Niebuhr suggests principles of value preference or value choice. These principles do not serve as criteria for establishing a scale of relative values that correspond to the scale of the Absolute Valuer. For the Absolute there is no scale because all beings are equally valued. They do, however, provide practical help to the Christian in the choices to be made. They are: (1) "Forget about your own value. You are beloved. You are saved." (2) "Serve the value which is in greatest need." (3) "Serve the values at hand—those near to you." But perhaps the most significant of those principles is the last: (4) "There is no value choice we make which must not be made in reliance on forgiveness because it involves sacrifice of the good." [55] Any decision among relative values that chooses one valued being over another is inevitable but tragic: "In all choice of value, one must remember that one is making a sacrifice of something sacred. Vicarious suffering is in the nature of things; one good thing is sacrificed for another." [56]

Niebuhr's discussion is therefore built around a dualism that sharply distinguishes everything that is good for God from all relative values. As finite, human judgments and human values are relative; humans cannot value as God values. For example, the smallpox virus, as part of creation, is good for God. Yet no conceivable human-centered system could ever judge it to be good for the human, because it does not "meet the needs" of the human. Nor could we from our finite perspective ever understand how the virus could be good for God.

The value center of radical monotheism in both its relativizing function and valuational function therefore does not positively inform value choices. It does shape our attitudes toward life; it enables us to meet all of being acceptingly and affirmatively. This may be considered a serious defect in Niebuhr's theory only insofar as a theory of value is judged merely by its contribution to our making better concrete daily decisions among relative competing values. Whether this is the true function of Niebuhr's value theory will be examined in chapter 7.

CHAPTER FIVE

Metaethical Considerations in Niebuhr's Value Theory

W E MUST NOW return to examine three further significant aspects of Niebuhr's value theory: (1) the relationship among the good, the right, and the fitting, (2) the metaethical position implicit in his theory, and (3) the theory's relation to the ideal observer theory.

1. THE GOOD, THE RIGHT, AND THE FITTING

There are two distinct yet interrelated facets of Niebuhr's analysis of the concepts of the good, the right, and the fitting. In one, these terms serve as the foci of three different interpretive metaphors of the moral life and are examined as alternative concepts for thinking about human action. In the other, they refer to different aspects within the situation of beings in relation, as this is conceived in Niebuhr's theory of value, and are defined in mutual dependence. The former facet of his analysis is best exemplified in *The Responsible Self*; the latter, in "The Center of Value."

The Robertson Lectures that Niebuhr delivered in 1960 at the University of Glasgow were posthumously published as *The Responsible Self*. They had as their intention the presentation of an alternative to the traditional teleological and deontological theories of moral action. Niebuhr calls his alternative theory variously "the ethics of responsibility," "the ethics of the fitting," and "*cathēkontic* [sic] ethics."

Teleological, deontological, and *cathēkontic* ethics all em-

ploy a central synecdoche; that is, they take some particular
part of human action and use it as an interpretive symbol
for the whole. The central synecdoche in teleological ethics
is, according to Niebuhr's analysis, the image of man-the-
maker:

> What is man like in all his actions? The suggestion
> readily comes to him that he is like an artificer who con-
> structs things according to an idea and for the sake of
> an end. Can we not apply to the active life as a whole
> the image we take from our technical working in which
> we construct wheels and arrows, clothes and houses and
> ships and books and societies? So not only common-
> sense thinking about ideals, and ends, and means, but
> much sophisticated philosophy has construed human
> existence.[1]

The central synecdoche operative in deontological ethics is
taken from human politics. It is the image of man-the-
citizen:

> We come to self-awareness if not to self-existence in the
> midst of *mores*, of commandments and rules, *Thou shalt*s
> and *Thou shalt not*s, of directions and permissions.
> Whether we begin with primitive man with his sense of
> *themis*, the law of the community projected outward
> into the total environment, or with the modern child
> with father and mother images, with repressions and
> permissions, this life of ours, we say, must take account
> of morality, of the rule of the mores, of the ethos, of the
> laws and the law, of heteronomy and autonomy, of self-
> directedness and other-directedness, of approvals and
> disapprovals, of social, legal, and religious sanctions.
> This is what our total life is like, and hence arise the
> questions we must answer: "To what law shall I consent,
> against what law rebel? By what law or system of laws
> shall I govern myself and others? How shall I adminis-

ter the domain of which I am the ruler or in which I participate in rule?"[2]

Niebuhr relates the concepts of the good and the right to these two synecdoches of human action:

> Those who consistently think of man-as-maker subordinate the giving of laws to the work of construction. For them the right is to be defined by reference to the good; rules are utilitarian in character; they are means to ends. . . . Those, however, who think of man's existence primarily with the aid of the citizen image seek equally to subordinate the good to the right; only right life is good and right life is no future ideal but always a present demand.[3]

Niebuhr is disturbed by this subordination, in the one case, of the good to the right and, in the other, of the right to the good. It leaves no way to reconcile the good and the right on equal terms and also leaves "a double theory, of which the two parts remain essentially unharmonized."[4] This is one of the reasons Niebuhr thinks a new synecdoche is appropriate.

Niebuhr gives two further reasons why the deontological and teleological approaches are inadequate for understanding the moral life: they fail as guides to action in social emergencies and in personal suffering. Social emergencies are situations "in which a community has had to meet a challenge," a challenge that thwarts progress toward sought-after ends and defies subsumption under existing laws. Niebuhr gives examples of such emergencies:

> The emergence of modern America out of the Civil War when measures were adopted in response to challenges that the founding fathers had not foreseen; the welfare-state decisions of the New Deal era in reaction to depression and the entrance of the nation into the

sphere of international politics in reaction to foreign wars despite all desire for isolation—such events give evidence in the social sphere of the extent to which active, practical self-definition issues from response to challenge rather than from the pursuit of an ideal or from adherence to some ultimate laws.[5]

Teleologists usually deal with such emergencies by suspending their efforts to attain the sought-after goals and substituting an interim ethics. Deontologists usually suspend their laws until the crisis has passed. Yet neither theorist is able to incorporate these suspensions into the theories; they remain as addenda.[6] Hence deontology and teleology are inadequate interpretive schemes in the face of unexpected crises.

Niebuhr's most poignant point against these two traditional synecdoches for the moral life is that they fail to address the problem of personal suffering. That failure is significant since "it is in the response to suffering that many and perhaps all men, individually and in their groups, define themselves, take on character, develop their ethos." Yet "because suffering is the exhibition of the presence in our existence of that which is not under our control, or of the intrusion into our self-legislating existence of an activity operating under another law than ours, it cannot be brought adequately within the spheres of teleological and deontological ethics, the ethics of man-the-maker, or man-the-citizen."[7]

Niebuhr therefore proposes a new synecdoche with which to understand human action. The metaphor he chooses arises out of the situation of human dialogue, in which one answers questions that are put by another. By using the metaphor of man-the-answerer,

we think of all our actions as having the pattern of what we do when we answer another who addresses us. To

73

be engaged in dialogue, to answer questions addressed to us, to defend ourselves against attacks, to reply to injunctions, to meet challenges—this is common experience. And now we try to think of all our actions as having this character of being responses, answers, to actions upon us.[8]

Niebuhr defines this new symbolism of responsibility by pointing to four elements within it: alteraction, attentive interpretation, the idea of the fitting, and accountability.[9] Alteraction is fundamental to the metaphor of man-the-answerer, for "our moral action presupposes an action prior to our own as an answer presupposes a question."[10] But our reaction to that alteraction takes place only as a result of our attentive interpretation:

> The mind is ever in dialogue with what is objective to it. It receives signs, attends to them and interprets them with the aid of images, symbols, theories, concepts; but these were learned in previous encounters and mediated by social language. It hears words and meanings in the sounds; see[s] images in the colors, the light and the shade; feels shapes in the resistances. Meanings, images, shapes, symbols are neither projected outwards, nor are they pure impressions made by objects. They have been formed in social and personal dialogue with objective otherness, and are subject to a constant modification and correction. With their aid we interpret what is being said to us or what is being done to us; with them we understand the alteraction.[11]

The third element in the idea of responsible action is the idea of the fitting. As we interpret the alteraction we must make a fitting response; it must "be suitable to, correspond to, fit into, the alteraction in such a way that the two form one whole."[12] Finally, there must be an accountability in re-

74

sponsive action. Such action must anticipate answers to its response:

> Responsible action . . . is action in a dialogue whose future course may be largely indeterminate. . . . Whether or not the anticipated reactions to his action take place, [the agent] stays in the dialogue; he does not quit the conversation as though the fitting answer completed what the other and what he had to say.[13]

The symbolism of responsibility, Niebuhr argues, is better able to make intelligible the problems of emergencies and suffering than are the images available in deontology or teleology. Since the ethics of responsibility sees the fundamental driving force behind all moral action as alteraction, something that happens to us from without, emergencies become not so much exceptions to as exemplifications of this root metaphor. And since the meaning of "to suffer" itself contains the idea of bearing or being acted upon by something, the image of responsibility also incorporates the idea of suffering much better than the alternative images.

Niebuhr believes the metaphor of responsibility also provides a way to understand the concepts of the good and the right without subordinating the one to the other. We must examine the second facet of his analysis of the good, the right, and the fitting—the way he employs these terms within his understanding of human action as responsible—to see why. However, Niebuhr avoids the subordination of the right to the good and the good to the right only by subordinating them both to the fitting.

In "The Center of Value" Niebuhr suggests that the fundamental observation of his relational value theory is

> that value is present wherever one existent being with capacities and potentialities confronts another existence that limits or completes or complements it. Thus,

75

first of all, value is present objectively for an observer in the fittingness or unfittingness of being to being.[14]

Good and evil are simply the positive and negative forms of value:

> Good is a term which not only can be but which—at least in the form of one of its equivalents—must be applied to that which meets the needs, which fits the capacity, which corresponds to the potentialities of an existent being. It is, in this sense, that which is "useful." Evil, on the other hand, is that which thwarts, destroys, or starves a being in its activities.[15]

Yet value appears, second of all, not only among existences in mutual relation but also in the situation "in which such existences are in a state of becoming," in which they "have not yet achieved their own internal possibilities of becoming good for others."[16] The distinction between these situations is important because Niebuhr uses the image of fittingness only in his description of the first. His attribution of fittingness only to the first situation of value does not, however, mean that fittingness is but a species of the good, because Niebuhr finally subordinates this second situation of value to the first. A being's realization of its own internal possibilities is itself good only as a result of that realization's being good for another being.[17] Internal states of the self are good only as they "fit" into the situation of beings in interaction. To understand what Niebuhr means by the good, then, is to understand what he means by the fitting.

Though fittingness is mentioned in "The Center of Value," Niebuhr's later works explain this concept more fully. Regrettably, his fullest treatments of it remain in manuscript form, though *The Responsible Self* contains his most thorough published discussion.

Fittingness for Niebuhr is an indefinable intuitive category. Its meaning is described ostensively in the examples he gives of it.

A key example of fittingness is the way an answer "fits" a question:

> The fitting, the suitable, the correspondent, the consentaneous, the congruous, the meet, reply to a question is one which so relates itself to the latter that the two parts of the dialogue form one meaningful whole. . . . A statement is meaningless for all those who do not have in mind the question to which it is an answer. When we try to understand the work of an author we do not make much progress unless we are able to say with some precision what the problems or the questions are which he is endeavoring to answer. Thus the fitting action is one which so meets alteraction that the two together form a whole in which the two parts derive meaning from each other. They are suited to each other; they correspond.[18]

Expanding the example of question and answer, he suggests that an action fits a situation "as a statement in a dialogue fits into a whole conversation. The act is fitting because it meets the situation and gives a kind of preliminary completion to it."[19] Similar analogies are used when he speaks of the fitting of a sentence into a paragraph into a book, a chord into a movement into a symphony, and a scientific fact into the history of science.[20]

Niebuhr also uses examples that involve broader spheres of human activity. He speaks of the way "the act of eating a common meal fits into the lifelong companionship of a family";[21] the way "fitting action on the part of an educator appears in the fact that his deeds must respond not only to the questions propounded to him by the science he is teaching—as in a subject-centered curriculum—nor only to the questions and problems posed by his students—as in a student-centered curriculum—but also into the interactions of his culture";[22] of the way fitting adjustments must be made to marriage partners;[23] and of the way a career choice must be "fitting to a man and to the situation in which he lives."[24]

One of his more interesting examples along this line is found in his unpublished manuscripts:

> The fitting action of a statesman is doubtless one which is congruent with his nation's past actions, with its constitutional decisions, with its movement toward survival in the future; it is also one which meets the alteraction and interaction of groups within the nation and of other nations on the basis of a "meet," a "true" interpretation of those actions. From the point of view of an ethics of the right, of obedience to laws, most political actions are regarded as of a compromise character; from the point of view of an ethics of ends as involving abandonment of the nation's purposes. But from the point of view of an ethics of responsibility they often appear to be fitting actions, which seek to insert the nation's activity into the total interaction of many nations in such a way that a continuing, value-conserving and value-creating process will result. When a nation, such as Great Britain in our times, abandons its purposes of building an empire and accepts a more modest role in the family of nations than it had been accustomed to play, its decision is challenged by those who identify the national purpose with empire-building and empire-maintaining. But from the viewpoint of responsibility ethics, its decisions to grant independence to India and to prepare Nigeria, for instance, for self-government may be approved as highly fitting, as corresponding not only to long British traditions but to the alteractions of Asian and African nations and to a total situation in human history.[25]

Niebuhr employs two further illustrations of fittingness, in craftsmanship and in driving:

> We may use an illustration from craftsmanship here, for craftsmanship is also a kind of doing which makes use of the idea of fitting in the midst of all its means-end reasoning. When a carpenter fits a tenon into a mortise he must see to it that the former meets the latter on all sides as well . . . as that it be of proper length. He does well, of course, if in doing this he follows the laws of making all sides square and of measuring carefully. But in the products of *old* craftsmanship we find many a mortise and tenon which fit exactly without conforming to such rules.[26]

Niebuhr recognizes that this analogy from craftsmanship is somewhat misleading, for "in his responsibility man has no such nicely fixed structures into which to insert his deeds." Therefore he suggests that

> a more apt comparison is that of the motor-car driver who must make forty decisions each minute. Neither obedience to rules of the road, nor desire to arrive at his goal, offers sufficient basis for his conduct.[27]

These analogies of the carpenter and the driver highlight a feature of Niebuhr's understanding of fittingness that those analogies deriving from the situation of dialogue between persons tend to obscure, namely its strongly deterministic character. For Niebuhr there is almost a structural context in which and to which the self reacts. That structure is precedent to the self's interpretation and response, and the self's task is to fit its reaction to the structure much as a carpenter crafts a tenon to fit into a given mortise. The impetus for action in Niebuhr's view is always action directed at the self from outside the self with impact on the self. The question the responsible self asks is not "What is my goal?" or "What is the law?" but "What is going on?" or "What is happening to me?"[28]

Niebuhr's relation to Stoic ethics is important in this regard. He acknowledges that his category of responsibility "is the category to which the Stoics gave the name of the '*kathekonta*,' that is, of 'things meet and fit.'"[29] Yet he is indebted to the Stoics for more than the category. Niebuhr finds the content of their ethics strikingly similar to his own:

> The Stoics are concerned with *nomos* and with the ideal life of apathy, or serenity. But primarily they deal with the ways men react, wisely or foolishly, to the things that befall them, to the things that are not in their power, to pain and pleasure, good and evil fortune. To respond to these things with passion is to react without understanding, without wisdom, without humanity. The secret of the wise life is its recognition of the presence in all events of universal Nature, of "creative, cosmic power, the world-thought," the world-reason. When birth and death and the things that happen to life between these terminal points are understood as outworkings of the world-reason, or of God, as the later Stoics said, then the wise man will do the fitting thing, the act that is in accord with the working of the universal reason. Stoic action is action in the universe; it is not dominated by the concerns of a single, individual life, nor yet by those of some special group. The Stoic is a citizen of the cosmos to whom nothing is foreign that is not foreign to the central, all-pervading power; he looks to every event as expressive in some fashion of universal plan and pattern; he interprets it in that way and so tries to respond fittingly.[30]

For both Niebuhr and the Stoics there is a structure in things, a kind of universal law; fitting action is action that conforms to that law and is consentaneous and congruous with it.[31]

The image of "the motor-car driver who must make forty decisions a minute" invokes the comparison of Niebuhr's view of fittingness with the thought of social behaviorism, because it brings to mind the stimulus-response character of action. The driver's actions respond to innumerable perceptual and kinesthetic stimuli as the driver maneuvers the car along the road. Some of the driver's reactions are the result of social stimuli, stimuli such as speed limit signs, traffic laws, and common-sense rules of the road. Niebuhr's thought has behavioristic tendencies because he interprets human action as a response to a stimulus, alteraction. However, his thought is distinguished from a Watsonian form of behaviorism in that the self's response that arises in reaction to alteraction is thoroughly social; it is a "response to an action upon him in accordance with his interpretation of the action and with his expectation of response to his response; and all of this is in a continuing community of agents."[32]

The behaviorism of George H. Mead is similar. Mead distinguishes his form of behaviorism from John B. Watson's by claiming that reactions are the result not of an externally imposed conditioned reflex but of a pattern of response socially learned and internalized by the subject. This distinction comes into play as Mead tries to understand language:

What I want to insist upon is that the process, by means of which these responses that are the ideas or meanings become associated with a certain vocal gesture, lies in the activity of the organism, while in the case of the dog, the child, the soldier, this process takes place, as it were, outside of the organism. The soldier is trained through a whole set of evolutions. He does not know why this particular set is given to him or the uses to which it will be put; he is just put through his drill, as an animal is trained in a circus. The child is similarly exposed to experiments without any thinking on his part. What thinking proper means is that this process of associating chair as object with the word "chair" is a process that human beings in society carry out, and then internalize. Such behavior certainly has to be considered just as much as conditioned behavior which takes place externally, and should be considered still more, because it is vastly more important that we should understand the process of thinking than the product of it.[33]

Similarly, the patterns of interpretation, images, and symbols of which Niebuhr speaks are internalized social meanings that structure the situation of response. As a result, the self's

responses in the present to encountered Thou's and It's are guided largely by the remembered, a priori patterns. It seeks to interpret each new occasion by assimilating it to an old encounter, and it tends to respond to the newly present in the way it had learned to answer its apparent counterparts in the past. The responsive, interpreting self is highly conservative not because it loves the past but because its interpretative equipment binds it to the past. The categories of its historical reason largely determine what it can now know and how it will respond.[34]

The deterministic character of Niebuhr's discussion of the fitting does not become so dominant that moral action becomes impossible. His view of the self invokes the image of a small figure upon whom multiple vectors or rays are converging, vectors representing the many alterations in the self's context.[35] The self's reaction or response, however, is determined to a degree by the self's interpretation of those many vectors. Yet the fitting response in any given context is not itself the result of the agent's choosing but belongs to the structure of the situation as it is interpreted by the agent.

Niebuhr therefore interprets freedom not as freedom to act but as freedom to choose our interpretation of the actions radiating upon us:

> The question of freedom arises in this connection as the question of the self's ability in its present to change its past and future and to achieve or receive a new understanding of its ultimate historical context. If these two modifications are possible, then reinterpretation of present action upon the self must result, and a new kind of reaction, a response that fits into another lifetime and another history, can and will take place.[36]

By reinterpreting the past, both social and personal, and revising our interpretation of the future, we are able to have a kind of freedom. Yet, says Niebuhr, "if we look in all this for the arbitrary free will, we can locate it only at the point where the agent commits himself to inquiry into the further, longer series of interactions and into the responses taking place in a larger society, or at the point where he commits himself to resolute questioning of the adequacy of his stereotyped, established interpretations."[37]

Niebuhr offers two different analyses of the right in relation to these understandings of the good and the fitting. In "The Center of Value," right is employed as the term applied to "that relation between beings, good-for-each-other, in which their potentiality of being good for each other is realized."[38] Its application thus depends on the distinction Niebuhr draws between the two situations in which value appears: that of existent beings in actual relation and that of beings "in a state of becoming, in which . . . they have not yet achieved their own internal possibilities of becoming

83

good for others."[39] For example, a being, A, can be said to be good for a being, B, insofar as A either presently meets or has the potential to meet B's needs. "Good" is in this way applied to beings in relation, though not to the relation. In contrast, "right" is applied to an actual relation. When A and B are related in such a way that A's potential goodness-for-B and B's potential goodness-for-A have become actual, then the relation AB can be said to be "right." Another way of putting this point is to say that beings are rightly related to each other when their actual relations conform to the structure of their actual needs.

Remarkable in Niebuhr's discussion of the right is his claim that his theory "can distinguish between the good and the right without reducing the one to the other or setting up two independent principles."[40] The reduction he wants to avoid constitutes one of his dissatisfactions with deontological and teleological theories. Yet it is hard to see how his own analysis avoids the reduction of the right to the good. His distinction between the right and the good rests on the definition of the right as mutual actual goodness. Insofar as this is the case, his own view is liable to the same criticism he makes of teleology's reduction of the right to the good.

However, in "The Responsible Self" manuscript Niebuhr develops an analysis of the right which does not define the right in terms of the good. He begins by noting that

in common meaning conduct is right when it conforms to law, whether the law be that of the conscience, or social will, or natural law in its political and ethical meaning, or the law of reason or God. But after that has been said the question inevitably arises about the basis of the law. If it is right to obey the right, i.e., the law, or if conduct must correspond to the law, what is it that makes a law right?[41]

The answer he gives to this question is that

84

the law is always a statement of what is fitting in a situation. When it does not express the fitness of a means to
a certain end, as in the case of the rule that one must
eat nourishing food if one wants to be healthy, then it
expresses some other kind of fittingness, such as that of
the way our actions must fit into those of our companions. . . . In general, the right as rule is a statement of
what people regard as fitting; not only as fitting into
the context of a single man's movement toward a goal
but as fitting into the interaction of all the agencies,
natural, human and supernatural which are involved in
interaction.[42]

The relation between the right and the expedient further
illuminates the way he defines the right by means of the
fitting:

In general, then, the situation with respect to our actions seems to be this: they are fitted into smaller or
larger contexts. We may ask about tomorrow's, next
year's, or the eternal consequences of an action; about
the fittingness of a political decision to the immediate
temper of the people or its fittingness in the nation's
history, or fittingness in an international interaction ex-
tending over the course of centuries. Statements about
what is fitting always, in all situations or in a universal
context we call statements of the right; those that fit
into less extensive patterns of interaction are usually
called expedient. The right is what is expedient in the
longest run, in view of all the agencies that are involved; the expedient is what is right in an immediate
response to alteraction and interaction without respect
to the larger context.[43]

There is a similarity in these two analyses of the right:
both depend on an ideal of a universal perspective from
which the relations between beings are most accurately

judged. In "The Responsible Self" manuscript this is evident in the right's being defined in terms of what is fitting in a universal context. Although not as obvious, it is also evident in "The Center of Value": if a judgment is to be made that two beings are indeed fulfilling their mutual potentialities of being good-for-each-other, some perspective must be assumed that could take into account the multidimensionality of relations in which beings find themselves. Implicit here is a reference to God's view of things, a reference that will be examined in the concluding section of this chapter.

2. NIEBUHR'S METAETHICAL NATURALISM

Niebuhr never himself pigeonholes his value theory into a metaethical classification, but an attempt to examine his theory in light of such a scheme is helpful in seeing what is at stake in his discussion of value.

One way to categorize ethical theories is to classify them as naturalistic, supernaturalistic, nonnaturalistic, or noncognitive.[44] Naturalistic theories define value terms in nonvalue terms. Normative terms are reduced to factual terms, usually observable and analyzable by the methods of science. Supernaturalistic theories also define value, only they do so in theological or metaphysical instead of factual terms. Nonnaturalistic theories argue that value is irreducible to factual or metaphysical terms but is directly intuited in itself. Noncognitivism, in contrast to these other ways, suggests that value judgments are not cognitive judgments at all, but are disguised expressions of attitudes, feelings, or commands.

Noncognitivism can be easily ruled out as a way of understanding Niebuhr's theory of value, for it rests on the view that value judgments have no cognitive meaning, that is, they are not assertions about anything which could be said to be true or false. Rather, they depend on the feelings, desires, and attitudes of the one who makes such claims. Yet

Niebuhr, as we have seen, argues for an "objective relativism" in value theory. Central to his theory is the claim that value is objective in precisely the sense that noncognitivists deny, namely in that value is present in the relations between beings whether the beings or anyone who is observing those beings feels, desires, or even thinks about value. Values have cognitive content; judgments about values can be made and assessed.[45]

Supernaturalism, like naturalism, is a definist theory of justification: value is defined in non-value terms. In its most characteristic form, supernaturalistic theory defines the right in terms of God's will: an act is right if it is commanded by God. However the good can be similarly defined: something is good if it is desired or willed by God.

Insofar as supernaturalism simply defines the good as "that which God desires," it fails to be fully descriptive of Niebuhr's discussion of relative values on two counts. First, Niebuhr defines the good, as we have seen, in terms of the fitting: "Good is a term which . . . must be applied to that which meets the needs, which fits the capacity, which corresponds to the potentialities of an existent being."[46] For Niebuhr the judgment that something fits a being's needs does not depend on knowing what God desires. Second, Niebuhr's theocentric relativism does not allow that the human could know God's desires per se, so that it prevents a direct relation of finite human judgments and absolute divine judgments. As we have seen, that whatever is, is good for God does not so much inform our own value judgments as relativize them.

Yet the question remains how Niebuhr justifies the assertion that whatever is, is good for God. In regard to this question the relation between Niebuhr and supernaturalism becomes less clear. The knowledge that whatever is, is good for God is for Niebuhr always a consequence of radical faith in the One beyond the many. His attack on value-theology in "Value-Theory and Theology" rests on his re-

87

jection of its claim that knowledge of the good is precedent to religious faith.[47] Knowledge of the good-for-God always comes after one has been given confidence in God by God. This priority is evident in the following passage: "Should it happen that confidence is given to me in the power by which all things are and by which I am; should I learn in the depths of my existence to praise the creative source, [then] I shall understand and see that, *whatever is, is good,* affirmed by the power of being, supported by it, intended to be, good in relation to the ultimate center, no matter how unrighteous it is in relation to finite companions."[48] If revelation is operative here, it is so at the level at which the confidence is given and not at a level at which the proposition "whatever is, is good for God" is revealed. Only the latter would constitute supernaturalism in the strict sense.

This is not to deny that Niebuhr's theory has strong affinities with supernaturalism. In the concluding paragraphs of "The Center of Value" Niebuhr makes this observation about monotheistic value theory:

> Its starting point, its dogmatic beginning, is with the transcendent One for whom alone there is an ultimate good and for whom, as the source and end of all things, whatever is, is good. It may indeed use a sort of psychological relativism at this point, since it cannot say that God has need of any being external to himself; hence it may be able only to say that whatever is exists because it pleases God. But whether the relation is to need or to desire, in any case the starting point is that transcendent absolute for whom, or for which, whatever is, is good.[49]

Having previously defined good in terms of objective needs, Niebuhr attempts in this passage to circumvent the correlate implication that what is good for God is that which meets God's needs. But Niebuhr's God as absolute and sovereign can have no needs.[50] He therefore invokes the psychological relativism that makes the good dependent on desire in trying to explain how things can be understood as being good for God. Accordingly, things exist because God desires them, or better, because they please God. The strong correlation here found among that which is good, that which exists, and that which God desires, cannot, however, be reduced to definitive identifications. The claim "whatever is exists because it pleases God" surely is not equivalent to the definition "'X is' means 'X pleases God.'" Nor would Niebuhr ever define "X is good" as "X pleases God." Yet if Niebuhr's theory were supernaturalistic, it would involve precisely such definitions. Hence, Niebuhr's theory is not best described as supernaturalist, though it has some affinities with such an approach.

The remaining metaethical theories are naturalism and nonnaturalism. Naturalism holds that value is definable in terms of facts—facts that can be observed and discovered on the basis of empirical principles. The nonnaturalist holds that value is not definable but is a directly intuited property of things: if one looks at something carefully and reflects on it, one immediately knows whether it is good. Hence goodness can only be ostensively described.

Insofar as a naturalistic or nonnaturalistic theory holds that value is a property simply attributable to beings, Niebuhr's relational theory fits neither. Niebuhr insists that value is not a characteristic of being but of beings in relation. Yet the basic thrusts of naturalism and nonnaturalism can be broadened to include the concern of Niebuhr's theory to maintain the relational character of value. It is not alien to Niebuhr's thought to see value as a "property" ascribable to beings in relation, even if value is not a property of beings simply considered. But then, what kind of relational property is value, natural or nonnatural?

The answer to this question depends on how "fittingness" is interpreted in Niebuhr's theory. Since both goodness and rightness are defined by Niebuhr in terms of his concept of fittingness, there can be no question that the good and the right are definable. But the conclusion that Niebuhr's theory is therefore naturalistic cannot be drawn until the status of fittingness is determined. If fittingness for Niebuhr is itself a value term and not reducible to some purely factual basis, then it is ultimately a form of nonnaturalism.

A nonnaturalistic interpretation is supported by the argument that fittingness is for Niebuhr an indefinable category, its meaning only clarified ostensively. However, intuitiveness alone is insufficient to make the case for nonnaturalism. It is also necessary that the quality that is intuited be uniquely moral or uniquely normative. Pleasantness is a good example of a simple, indefinable property: we either directly sense, or intuit, something as pleasant or not. Yet it is an empirical property nonetheless because it rests on psychological states. If the good is defined as that which is pleasant (as it is in most forms of hedonism), then to determine if something is good is simply to observe if it causes pleasant feelings in me or in others.

Is fittingness such a property of beings in relation? Fittingness differs from pleasantness in its objectivity: it is not for Niebuhr primarily a psychological state but an apprehended quality of the relations between beings. As his examples of fittingness show—examples such as the way a carpenter fits a mortise into a tenon and the way drivers "fit" their actions into the situations they confront as they progress[51]—fittingness is applicable to situations broader than the normative and moral. Therefore, it cannot be classified as a uniquely moral or normative quality of relations, and hence Niebuhr's theory is best understood as a species of naturalism.[52]

It is a naturalism, however, greatly informed by Niebuhr's socio-historical relativism. Fittingness depends to a large extent upon the interpretation given to alteration. The patterns of interpretation with which we come to our experience are themselves the product of our socio-historical past:

Not with timeless ideas, recollected in Platonic recall of the soul's participations in the eternal; not with timeless laws of never-changing nature or of a pure human, un-historical reason, does the self come to its present en-counters. It comes rather with images and patterns of interpretation, with attitudes of trust and suspicion, ac-cumulated in its biographical and historical past. It comes to its meetings with the Thou's and It's with an a priori equipment that is the heritage of its personal and social past; and it responds to the action of these others in accordance with the interpretations so made possible.[53]

A judgment about a thing's fittingness, hence, is not objec-tively absolute, as if it were the product of pure perception or pure reason. It depends on an interpretive context, and such contexts are always relative to a socio-historical reason.

This fact however does not militate against our interpret-ing Niebuhr's theory as naturalistic, because Niebuhr's epis-temological position places empiricism in precisely the same socio-historical context. Value theory, he says, "is then rela-tivistic . . . in the sense in which physical science is relativis-tic without loss of objectivity."[54] There is no uninterpreted experience, either moral or empirical: "Bare sense experi-ence unmixed with rational elements is inaccessible to us; reason forms and interprets sense experience; experience validates or invalidates such experienced-filled reason-ing."[55] This socio-historical character of even our empirical interpretations does not, however,

mean that we cannot correct indefinitely in the course of the continuing dialogues with nature and with each other the ideas, concepts, relations we have taken on trust. It does mean that an element of believing, of ac-ceptance of the reports of our companions, of the tra-dition of our society about encounters with nature, en-ters into all our knowing at the very beginning.[56]

Because the socio-historical character of value discourse does not differentiate it from empirical discourse, and because the socio-historical character of both does not for Niebuhr militate against either's objectivity, his view of the socio-historical character of reason does not prevent the interpretation of his theory as naturalistic.[57]

3. NIEBUHR AND THE IDEAL OBSERVER THEORY

Niebuhr, as we have seen, draws a sharp distinction between absolute values, defined as what is good for God, and all relative values, defined as what is good for some finite being. Because of this distinction, Niebuhr has difficulty directly relating God as the Center of Value to human value choices. God in his theory functions more as a relativizer of all finite values than as a standard against which mutually to compare them.

Though Niebuhr denies any *explicit* connections between God's valuing and human valuing, are there *implicit* ones at work in his thought? One way of making such connections would be through what has come to be known in philosophy as the ideal observer theory. Though Niebuhr's view has certain affinities with this theory of the meaning of ethical and valuational terms, it is significantly different from it. Comparing the two approaches, however, is a helpful heuristic device for further understanding the implicit connection between the Absolute Valuer and human valuation in Niebuhr's thought.

The ideal observer theory is an absolutist and dispositional analysis of ethical and value statements. Roderick Firth in his essay "Ethical Absolutism and the Ideal Observer" characterizes it as "the kind of analysis . . . which would construe statements of the form 'x is P,' in which P is some particular ethical predicate, to be identical in meaning with statements of the form: 'Any ideal observer would react to x in such and such a way under such and such conditions.'"[58] It is absolutist in that it "implies that ethical statements are true or false, and consistent or inconsistent with one another, without special reference to the people who happen to be asserting them."[59] It is dispositional in that "a certain being (or beings) either actual or hypothetical, is (or are) disposed to react to something in a certain way."[60] Firth emphasizes that this type of analysis does not depend on the existence of an actual being having the characteristics of an ideal observer, but only on the conceivability of such a being. Hence the meaning of ethical statements can be logically specified in terms of an ideal observer whether or not that observer exists. Firth's theory thus holds that the meaning of ethical statements does not depend on the existence of experiencing subjects. Because of this, it is an objectivist analysis.

Firth notes that the ideal observer theory understands value relationally, i.e., "it construes ethical terms in such a way that to apply an ethical term to a particular thing (e.g., an act), is to assert that that thing is related in a certain way to some other thing, either actual or hypothetical,"[61] a view that is especially interesting in light of our study of Niebuhr's theory of value.

Firth lists six characteristics of such an ideal observer: (1) He is omniscient with respect to non-ethical facts. (2) He is omnipercipient. (3) He is disinterested. (4) He is dispassionate. (5) He is consistent. And (6) in other respects he is normal.[62]

A comparison of Niebuhr's theory with Firth's must begin by determining if Niebuhr's is an absolutist view. According to Firth, the issue pivots around the question whether "ethical statements are true or false, and consistent or inconsistent with one another, without special reference to the people who happen to be asserting them."[63] For Niebuhr value is always relative to some being in relation to which the value is a value-for. Values are not absolute in the sense that they can be defined absolutely in themselves; value has

93

no meaning apart from beings for whom other beings are values. This means that the proposition "x is good" within Niebuhr's system must be further specified "x is good for y" before any judgment can be made on its truth. However, this does not militate against Niebuhr's position being absolutist in Firth's sense because the reference that an absolutist analysis must preclude is a "special reference to the people that happen to be asserting them" and not a reference to another being in relation to whom the first is of value. And this relation is as objective to an observer as are the beings who are so related.[64] Hence Niebuhr's theory can be considered absolutist in Firth's terms.

Yet Niebuhr's theory differs significantly from Firth's in that his analysis is not dispositional. For Firth, the meaning of ethical terms finally depends on their reference to psychological dispositions of one sort or another; he is able to avoid the subjectivist implications usually associated with dispositional approaches by defining the dispositions as belonging to a hypothetically conceivable and not to an actually existing being. Niebuhr's analysis depends on neither the dispositions of a hypothetical, nor those of an actually existing being. Value for Niebuhr is a structural category, dependent on the given structures of beings-in-relation. It is indeed "objectively present for an observer in the fittingness or unfittingness of being to being,"[65] but in no way depends on the dispositions of that observer. Rather the observer merely perceives the value structurally present in the relation.

Even though Niebuhr's discussion of value cannot be understood as a form of the ideal observer theory, it does implicitly appeal to an interpretive perspective that is almost defined in the same way as that of the ideal observer. In Niebuhr's epistemology the point of view or the standpoint is significant: "What is accessible and knowable is so only from a certain point of view and in a certain relation."[66] This is true with regard to God as well as the human. The only difference is that God's is the universal and inclusive

94

standpoint whereas the human's is only fragmentary and partial.

God's standpoint is, first of all, universal. Human knowing is always limited by the historic reason that furnishes the interpretive patterns and symbols which make knowing possible. According to Niebuhr, we see an objective world before us, but see it always through the socio-historical spectacles without which we would not see at all. God's knowing, however, is direct and immediate; God has no need of interpretive structures. The analogy to a perceptual standpoint is strong in the following passage in which Niebuhr relates God's point of view to the church's view of itself:

> The church's external history of itself may be described as an effort to see itself with the eyes of God. The simultaneous, unified knowledge from within and from without that we may ascribe to God is indeed impossible to men, but what is simultaneous in his case can in a measure be successive for us. The church cannot attain an inclusive, universal point of view but it can attempt to see the reflection of itself in the eyes of God.[67]

Other expressions used for this all-encompassing standpoint are "the transcendent and disinterested point of view," the "absolute standpoint," and "a universal point of view."[68]

God's standpoint is also disinterested. Sometimes this disinterestedness is stated so strongly that it sounds almost nihilistic: "All the relative judgments of worth," writes Niebuhr, "are equalized in the presence of this One who loves all and hates all, but whose love like whose hatred is without emotion, without favoritism."[69] Yet it is also described in more positive terms as a universal interestedness: God is described as "an impartial spectator . . . whose impartiality is that of loyalty to the universal cause."[70] God's disinterest is God's universal interest in whatever is, since for God, whatever is, is good.

Thus, Niebuhr uses this image of a universal, disinterested

95

standpoint to bridge provisionally the gap between our relative value judgments and God's valuations: the more universal and disinterested our standpoint, the better our judgments will be. The gap does remain, however, and humans are still not able to value as God values. Yet the image of the universal, disinterested observer serves as a kind of guy line, shot across the chasm, that gives humans some way of striving to make better judgments.

In several examples Niebuhr appeals to a universal, disinterested point of view as an ideal goal for human judgments. He criticizes the standpoint we usually take as "interested men":

> We were and are unable to achieve the single-mindedness of impersonal science in our moral thinking and acting not because we could and cannot be impersonal here but because we would and will not look at things from the viewpoint of a universal person. It is always an interested morality, a wishful and idolatrous and corrupted one which we employ apart from God.[71]

The implication is that if we took such a viewpoint we might achieve the single-mindedness of impersonal science in our moral reflection.

Another passage that employs this ideal of a disinterested point of view is found in "The Center of Value." Niebuhr suggests that though desire is necessary in the moral life insofar as it moves us to do the good, "desire uncriticized by a rational nonparticipating, disinterested point of view of the relations of being to being is as subject to error as is sensation without rational interpretation."[72]

And finally, a third example can be found in Niebuhr's response to his brother's criticism of his position on the Japanese invasion of Manchuria: "But this same structure in things which is our enemy is our redeemer; 'it means intensely and means good'—not the good which we desire, but the good which we would desire if we were really good

96

and really wise."[73] In all these examples, Niebuhr appeals to a universal, disinterested point of view, a view which serves as an ideal toward which our human judgments should strive but which is never fully achievable, since as finite beings we are always limited by our partial and fragmentary knowledge.

This ideal of a universal, disinterested point of view is similar to the ideal striven after in science. Unlike Firth's ideal observer, Niebuhr's ideal point of view does not depend in any sense on moral or normative dispositions. The universal, disinterested point of view which is definitive of God's perspective simply sees things as they really are, unburdened by the interpretive structures essential to human knowing. Such a perspective is able to see how things really fit, how they are really good, because it sees things simply as they really are, which is to say how they are for God:

> The ultimate nature of an event is not what it is in its isolation only but what it is in its connection with all other events, not what it is for itself but also what it is from an inclusive point of view. The event, as it really is, is the event as it is for God who knows it at the same time and in one act from within as well as from without, in its isolation as well as in its community with all other events.[74]

There is a tension between, on the one hand, Niebuhr's sharp distinction of all relative values from the absolute values of the good-for-God in such a way that the two are separated by the unbridgeable gap between finite and infinite, and, on the other hand, his hints of a universal, disinterested point of view as a standard by which to judge our human knowledge and values. If the gap is truly unbridgeable, then all relative values are equally valid (or invalid) in a universal context. But, as has been shown, such a position is problematic with regard to comparative judgments. However, a more implicit undercurrent swells along just under the surface of Niebuhr's thought and hints of a standard for judgments in the ideal of a universal, disinterested point of view.

Niebuhr never reconciles these two approaches. The tension is nonetheless creative in his thought. It enables his theological reflection on value to go beyond the critical, relativizing function to which it appears to be limited in "The Center of Value" to a position where it makes at least tentative moves towards being "an aid in accuracy of action."

CHAPTER SIX

God and Value
in Niebuhr's Theology

OUR STUDY up to this point has primarily focused on Niebuhr's value theory from a philosophical perspective. I have tried to show how Niebuhr explicitly develops that theory and to indicate its presuppositions and implications. We must now broaden our investigation to include the role of value in his specifically Christian thought. As I suggested at the outset, one of Niebuhr's unique contributions to twentieth-century Christian theology is the way that he makes value considerations indispensable to an adequate understanding of Christian faith in God.

1. CHRISTIAN FAITH AS VALUATION

Christian faith is for Niebuhr primarily an affair of valuation. What one comes to when one comes to faith is not a knowledge of objects, supernatural or natural, that were previously unknown; nor does one discover or see revealed the being of God, unknown before the onset of faith. Instead, the being which persons confront as the ultimate limit of their lives is shown to be good, trustworthy, and faithful—in short, to be a person. Hence

the content of revelation is not the self-disclosure of an unknown being, but the unveiling of the value of a known being. What is revealed in revelation is not a being as such, but rather its deity-value, not that it is, but that it "loves us," "judges us," that it makes life worth living.[1]

Niebuhr's view of faith as valuation presupposes his understanding of natural religion, and his view of natural religion rests on his understanding of generic human faith. For Niebuhr some form of faith, some trust in and loyalty to beings, is definitive of the very nature of selfhood. Niebuhr finds it "evident, when we inquire into ourselves and our common life, that without . . . active faith or . . . reliance and confidence on power we do not and cannot live."[2] Faith, however, can be negative as well as positive. In its negative form, faith is distrust in and disloyalty to the beings on whom we find ourselves dependent. When Niebuhr explores "natural religion," he turns to the negative form of faith, for the natural religion of distrust forms the backdrop for our lives as selves prior to revelation. "In our actual situation . . . what we see is never faith in its pure positive form but in a negative or distorted form of distrust and disloyalty."[3]

Niebuhr's most thorough discussion of natural religion appears in his unpublished manuscript "Faith on Earth," under the chapter title "Broken Faith." Two main points are made prior to this chapter: (1) that faith is an activity essential to selves and is a generic phenomenon, and (2) that the structure of faith is triadic and always involves a reference to a third beyond those holding faith in each other. From this point he sets out the program for his chapter on broken faith:

> Our procedure therefore must be this, that we now use the understanding we have gained of the general structure of faith in interpersonal life for the sake of analyzing, as best we may, that faith in God of which we are conscious in ourselves in the company of the faithful. What we become aware of first of all when we direct our attention to it is that it has always been present

to us in a negative form and is now so present to us. Faith in God is the accompaniment of our existence as selves but first of all it is a dark background; it is present negatively as distrust and fear and hositility.[4]

This natural faith, this distrust in God is grounded in the discovery that "the self . . . finds itself to be absolutely dependent in its existence, completely contingent, inexplicably present in its here-ness and now-ness."[5] We first come to know God as that which throws us into being:

We are in the grasp of a power that neither asks our consent before it brings us into existence nor asks our agreement to continue us in being beyond our physical death. Sooner or later we awake to the realization that this is the way things are. . . . [Only] one thing I seem to know: I am I in this now and I am up against that which has matched me with this time and this time with me, I am up against *that which is*, and without which I am not.[6]

Niebuhr poignantly describes the reality that we are up against in his essay "Faith in Gods and in God":

What is it that is responsible for this passing, that dooms our human faith to frustration? We may call it the nature of things, we may call it fate, we may call it reality. But by whatever name we call it, this law of things, this reality, this way things are, is something with which we all must reckon. We may not be able to give a name to it, calling it only the "void" out of which everything comes and to which everything returns, though that is also a name. But it is there—the last shadowy and vague reality, the secret of existence by virtue of which things come into being, are what they are, and pass away. Against it there is no defense. This reality, this nature of things, abides when all else passes.

101

It is the source of all things and the end of all. It surrounds our life as the great abyss into which all things
plunge and as the great source whence they all come.
What it is we do not know save that it is and that it is the
supreme reality with which we must reckon.[7]

This distrust of the One from whom or from which everything comes ramifies deeply into all existence. It not only
infects our relation to the One beyond the many, it also
turns us against ourselves and each other. "Here," writes
Niebuhr, "disloyalty and distrust, self and neighbor, are so
involved that the distrust of God is a response to the companion's deception or disloyalty and the self's disloyalty in
[the] breaking of its promise is a source of its distrust." He
continues:

The great disorder of our existence cannot be elimi-
nated by a return to the innocence of a life in which
there is no promise and no loyalty and therefore neither treason or deceit. We are fated to be loyal and to
live by trust but all our loyalty appears only in the corrupted form of broken promises, and our trust in the
perverse form of the great suspicion that we are being
deceived.[8]

Hence our natural religion, our natural faith, and our natural mind leave us no way to break out of the vicious circle of
distrust and disloyalty.

Thus, Niebuhr's view of natural religion is essentially
negative. For many of his theological contemporaries, natural religion was a positive starting point for discussion of
Christian faith. In the "Chicago School" of thought, theologians like Henry Nelson Wieman were attempting to use
the human's "natural mind" as a basis for theological reflection. Yet in "Faith on Earth" the human's natural mind and
its natural religion are impediments to rather than starting

points for Christian faith. Human disloyalty, the form in which natural religion manifests itself, is human sin.[9]

Further, when Niebuhr speaks of "natural religion" he has in mind the role of human faith in the lives of selves prior to the faith won in revelation. Niebuhr is interested less in God's manifestation in nature than in the way God becomes known to selves in their history. Thus "natural religion" relates in Niebuhr's thought more to sociological and anthropological than to physical and empirical aspects of our existence in the world.

But there is a tension in Niebuhr's thought as a whole regarding his view of natural religion. In "Faith on Earth" Niebuhr argues that the only kind of loyalty we find among selves apart from explicit faith in God is the negative form, disloyalty. He recognizes that we are able to see this fact only from the perspective of reconciliation; nevertheless he suggests that it is a true depiction of the human condition. As we shall see below, it is the Christian's confession that through revelation a reestablishment of trust and loyalty is made possible. But apart from such revelation, according to Niebuhr, "all our loyalty appears only in the corrupted form of broken promises, and our trust in the perverse form of the great suspicion that we are being deceived."[10]

This analysis of natural religion seems to contradict the thrust of a good portion of the rest of Niebuhr's work, much of which depends on his analysis of a common human structure of faith found in trust and loyalty between selves, i.e., of faith in a positive sense. It is true that he never takes that analysis so far as to argue from the reality and presence of faith between selves to the reality of the object of radically monotheistic faith; that would be to suggest what he at one point rejects—a "pistological argument for the existence of God."[11] But his arguments in *Radical Monotheism and Western Culture* and *The Responsible Self* rest on an understanding of human existence in which trust and loyalty are fundamentally present in their positive forms as well as their negative.

Possibly the solution to this seeming contradiction could be found in Niebuhr's confessionalism. He never intended to be anything other than a Christian trying to reason about his faith. His arguments in *Radical Monotheism* and in *The Responsible Self* must be viewed therefore in this light. When he speaks of trust and loyalty in those works, he speaks from the standpoint of a Christian believer, having been reconciled to God and trying to make sense of that reconciliation. Any attempt to see his discussion as a general anthropological analysis of the self, is distorted at the outset and leads to the mistaken view that there is a contradiction between those works and his analysis of broken faith.

Some such argument might well be advanced; it would be difficult to point to specific passages that would either conclusively refute or confirm it. But the kinds of argument that Niebuhr presents throughout his work have to be seen as intelligible to a wider audience than merely Christian believers, for he intended to understand not simply Christian life but "human life from a Christian point of view."[12] Niebuhr's theory of the self, for example, is surely misunderstood if it is viewed as either a theory of the Christian self or a Christian theory of the self. It is a theory of the self that happens to be developed by a Christian for the purpose of better understanding what it means to be human in the world. Hence the contradiction remains.

The movement from distrust in and disloyalty to that reality from which we come and to which we go, to faith in that reality as God, is the center around which Niebuhr's understanding of Christian faith revolves. This movement is precisely the meaning and content of Christian faith—a fact attested to by his defining key terms within the Christian tradition by means of this movement, terms such as "conversion."[13] "revelation,"[14] "salvation,"[15] "redemption,"[16] "reformation,"[17] and "*metanoia*."[18]

The movement is not one from ignorance to knowledge. Nor does it impose upon the human new moral laws. Yet "it does involve the radical reconstruction of all our beliefs,"[19] because it demands a reinterpretation of our understanding of the total context in which we act and are acted upon. What is reconstructed is not the recognition of the powers that press in upon us and determine us; it is not that we come to see as unreal what we before thought was real. Rather, the realities that were and are there, are transvalued. Instead of being seen as threat, they are seen as gift; instead of being viewed as limits, they are potentialities; instead of being interpreted as fateful, they are salvific. In short, they are seen as personal rather than impersonal, and as good rather than indifferent or bad.

It cannot be overemphasized that the transvaluation that comes into play in the movement from distrust to trust is not transexistential; that is, faith does not give us a different ontology. Our interpretation of that ontology differs and is the locus of the movement of faith. This point is brought out by Niebuhr in an address to the American History Association:

> I will not undertake to defend the actuality of the object of theology—man before God and God before men. The definition of what is meant by "God" in that phrase is at least as complex and difficult as the definition of *nature* in the case of natural sciences, of *society* in the case of the social sciences. That men's ideas of what they confront in the determination of their destiny, in the why and wherefore of their existence, vary widely is well known; that what the believer calls God is called Fate or Chance by the unbeliever; or sometimes Life or Nature, we all know. Ideas of nature also vary widely, yet we assume that men live in and before the same nature, no matter how widely their interpretations of it and hence their responses to it differ.[20]

Niebuhr borrows an image from Alfred North Whitehead to elucidate this movement when he speaks of it as the transition from God the enemy to God the friend.[21] "God"

is a term applied to Being, both before and after the transvaluation of faith. The being which we in our natural religion distrust

> is present to us there as enemy. The natural mind is en-
> mity to God; or to our natural mind the One intention
> in all intentions is animosity. We live and move and
> have our being in a realm that is not nothingness but
> that is ruled by destructive power, which brings us and
> all we love to nothing.[22]

But through faith we come to count on God as friend, so
that Niebuhr is able to say: "The establishment of this friend-
ship [between God and man] is to me the key problem in
human existence."[23]

At other points, Niebuhr reserves the appellation "God"
to refer to the One only after the transvaluation of faith has
occured: "When we say that the power by which we are is
God, we may express our interpretation in trust, for to say
'God' is to say 'good' in our common speech; the word, God,
means the affirmer of our being, not its denier; 'God' means
the concern of the ultimate for what issues from it, not its
heedlessness or its animosity."[24] Whether the term be used
in the wider sense that speaks of the movement from seeing
God as enemy to seeing God as friend, or in the narrower
sense that limits it to refer to the One only as transvalued by
faith, the important point is that it is applied not to a new
being that was not there before but to the same being now
reinterpreted as having "the value of deity."[25]

The transvaluation of the whole context of one's self and
one's action is for Niebuhr not something that the human
accomplishes on its own, but is something that happens to it.
Niebuhr can only describe radically monotheistic faith as
"the gift of confidence in the principle of being itself, as the
affirmation of the real, as loyalty—betrayed and reconstructed many times—to the universe of being."[26] Indeed,
conversion to faith presupposes a transvaluation of the self

as the genesis of the self's transvaluation of its context. "The valuation of which man becomes aware in religious experience is not first of all his evaluation of a being," writes Niebuhr, "but that being's evaluation of him. Such a value-experience is primitive and original."[27] He expresses the same point in *The Meaning of Revelation*:

> Revelation means that we find ourselves to be valued rather than valuing and that all our values are transvaluated by the activity of a universal valuer. When a price is put upon our heads, which is not our price, when the unfairness of all the fair prices we have placed on things is shown up; when the great riches of God reduce our wealth to poverty, that is revelation.[28]

Because of this issue, Niebuhr breaks from even those forms of liberalism that were congenial to his own early thought. Niebuhr, it must be remembered, was the doctoral student of D. C. Macintosh. Macintosh, trained in the "Chicago school" of Christian liberalism, influenced Niebuhr's view of realism in religious knowledge, and strains of his empirical approach can be detected throughout the corpus of Niebuhr's work.[29] Yet in an article that Niebuhr contributed to a festschrift for Macintosh, he criticizes Macintosh's, as well as Henry Nelson Wieman's, theology not for being valuational but for basing religious valuation on values known prior to the experience of revelation. "They assume," Niebuhr says, "that men have a knowledge of absolutely valid values which is not only independent of their knowledge of God but which is also in some way determinative of God."[30] In contrast, Niebuhr advocates "the complete abandonment of an approach from values known as absolute prior to the experience of God,"[31] though he well recognizes that abandoning this approach does not mean abandoning the understanding that faith is primarily valuational. He sees that "it is possible and necessary to interpret religion as an affair of *valuation* without assuming that such valuation must or can be made on the basis of a previously established standard of values."[32] But the valuation that is primary in faith is the self's sense that it is valued by something beyond itself and not its own valuing.[33]

If the movement from distrust to trust of being is the center around which Niebuhr's understanding of radical faith revolves, then the spindle which supports that center is his view of Jesus Christ. When Niebuhr asks what grounds the possibility of such faith, he can only confess that for him as a Christian that possibility has been opened up by Jesus Christ:

> Jesus Christ is for me, as for many of my fellow Christians, the one who lived and died and rose again for this cause of bringing God to men and men to God and so also of reconciling men to each other and to their world. The establishment of this friendship is to me the key problem in human existence. Because through Jesus Christ—his fate—as well as by him—that is, his ministry—this has become evident to me; because in him I see the prospect of my own reconciliation; because I have been challenged to make this cause my own—therefore I call myself a Christian.[34]

This is not to say that radical faith is possible only through Jesus Christ. Niebuhr is careful to avoid exclusivist claims for Christ. "I do not have the evidence," he says, "which allows me to say that the miracle of faith in God is worked only by Jesus Christ and that it is never given to men outside the sphere of his working."[35] But Niebuhr must in his own life ascribe the possibility to Jesus Christ, for that is his confession of how he came to have confidence in the principle of being.

Niebuhr nowhere develops a fully articulated Christology, partly due to the fact that he was primarily a Christian ethicist and not a dogmatic theologian. It is also due partly to the fact that for him the Christ event is inexplicable. The very fact that Jesus Christ is able to bring about such a revolution in our valuation causes Niebuhr's only appeal, in all his work, to absurdity and irrationality rather than to reasoned reflection as a norm for thought:

> What is the absurd thing that comes into our moral history as existential selves, but the conviction, mediated by a life, death, and a miracle beyond understanding, that the source and ground and government and end of all things—the power we (in our distrust and disloyalty) call fate and chance—is faithful, utterly trustworthy, utterly loyal to all that issues from it? That it is not merely loyal to loyalty but loyal to the disloyal, not merely trustworthy by the loyal but also by the disloyal? To metaphysical thinking the irrational thing is the incarnation of the infinite, the temporalizing of the absolute. But this is not the absurdity to our existential, subjective, decision-making thought. What is irrational here is the creation of faith in the faithfulness of God by the crucifixion, the betrayal of Jesus Christ, who was utterly loyal to Him. . . . This is a greater surd: that the man who reasoned otherwise [than as one distrustful of the Creator], who counted on the faithfulness of God in keeping all the promises given to life, and who was loyal to all to whom he trusted God to be loyal, should come to his shameful end, like all the rest of us; and that, in consequence of this, faith in the God of his faith should be called forth in us.[36]

However, in *The Responsible Self* Niebuhr does hint at lines along which a Christology might be developed. Christ functions according to Niebuhr in two ways:

> On the one hand he appears as the perfect illustration or the incarnate pattern, as the first and only Christian.

On the other hand his personal, historical action is understood as God's way of making what is impossible for men possible.[37]

In the first function Jesus is seen as the exemplification of the incarnation of radically monotheistic faith: "The greatness of his confidence in the Lord of heaven and earth as fatherly in goodness toward all creatures, the consistency of his loyalty to the realm of being, seem unqualified by distrust or by competing loyalty."[38] This man is unique not because of something he *is* but something he does: "He is the responsible man who in all his responses to alterations did what fitted into the divine action."[39] In the second function Jesus makes possible for Christians radical trust in the One:

> Jesus Christ . . . is also the one who accomplishes in them this strange miracle, that he makes them suspicious of their deep suspicion of the Determiner of Destiny. He turns their reasoning around so that they do not begin with the premise of God's indifference but of his affirmation of the creature, so that the *Gestalt* which they bring to their experiences of suffering as well as of joy, of death as well as of life, is the *Gestalt*, the symbolic form, of grace.[40]

Exactly how this happens, how this is brought about, "Christians cannot easily say," but behind the mystery "the fact remains: the movement beyond resignation to reconciliation is the movement inaugurated and maintained in Christians by Jesus Christ"[41]

This transvaluation of the source of existence from a being worthy of distrust to a trustworthy being affects all relative evaluations. That is, faith transforms my perceptions of the relative values about me:

> All my specific and relative evaluations expressed in my interpretations and responses are shaped, guided, and

formed by the understanding of good and evil I have *upon the whole.* In distrust of the radical action by which I am, by which my society is, by which this world is, I must find my center of valuation in myself, or in my nation, or in my church, or in my science, or in humanity, or in life. Good and evil in this view mean what is good for me and bad for me; or good and evil for my nation, or good and evil for one of these other finite causes, such as mankind, or life, or reason. But should it happen that confidence is given to me in the power by which all things are and by which I am; should I learn in the depths of my existence to praise the creative source, [then] shall I understand and see that, *whatever is, is good*, affirmed by the power of being, supported by it, intended to be, good in relation to the ultimate center, no matter how unrighteous it is in relation to finite companions. And now all my relative evaluations will be subjected to the continuing and great correction. They will be made to fit into a total process producing good—not what is good for me (though my confidence accepts that as included), nor what is good for man (though that is also included), nor what is good for the development of life (though that also belongs in the picture), but what is good for being, for universal being, or for God, center and source of all existence.[42]

In this passage lies the key to the way Niebuhr envisions the relation between faith and relative valuation. His attempt in "The Center of Value" to develop philosophically the theory of value implicit in his theology leaves the radically monotheistic value center functioning more as a critical principle than as a positive point of reference for comparative judgments. He is not, of course, trying to develop a philosophical theory in complete detachment from his theological concerns and commitments. Nevertheless he focuses on the philosophical implications of his theory and does not appeal to the religious experience of being valued by God.

Hence the claim of radically monotheistic faith that whatever is, is good for God, is left without the experiential basis so crucial for its positive actualization in the self's decisions.

Yet even in the transvaluation of faith, God as the center of value does not provide a positive point of reference for comparative value judgments. Coming to faith does not change what is good for the human, what is good for life, or what is good for any other relative being; as we have seen, value for Niebuhr is a structural category dependent on the needs of beings. As part of the given conditions of life and of reality, those needs can no more change as a result of faith than can the reality of the beings related through them. What is good for a person does not depend on whether or not the person has faith in the source of being. Faith in God therefore does not directly change any of our relative valuations nor provide a principle with which to discriminate among relative values.

It does transform the attitude with which we approach all our relative valuations, for it transvalues the total context in which we exist. The idea of God as the center of value functions in Niebuhr's value theory per se (as that theory is presented in "The Center of Value") as a critical relativizing principle, reminding us that all our finite valuations and judgments are relative. In Niebuhr's theology, because the center is defined more primarily as that which values us, it also functions in the more positive role of enabling us to make all our relative judgments and relative valuations in the confidence that behind them stands the judgment and the valuation of the Absolute Valuer for whom whatever is, is good. The structures of being are not transformed, so that whatever is, has become good for us; but, rather, we come to understand that whether something is good for us is irrelevant to its being good for God. *Whatever is, is good for God.* That is the central valuation for radical faith. Obviously we shall never be able to say, for instance, that the smallpox virus is good for the human. We shall, however, have to say that it is good for God. But in saying the latter, the attitude with which we say the former is transformed. At that crucial point, for Niebuhr, faith transforms our relative valuations.

Niebuhr defined this transformed attitude in his Christian ethics lectures under the topic "Response to the Creative Action of God." For Niebuhr, the doctrine of creation itself expresses "the respect for being, the affirmation of what is, the positive valuation of existent reality."[43] When he speaks of the Christian response to creation he outlines four components of this transformed attitude. It is first "at its minimum the response of sheer *acceptance*." The attitude then proceeds from acceptance to affirmation: "It is world-affirmative. It says 'yes' to existence." After acceptance and affirmation comes understanding. Niebuhr describes this third step by analogy, showing how these first three stages of response are present in the act of viewing a piece of modern art:

> I may simply reject Picasso's later work by thoughtlessly interpreting it as the work of a bad creator. It ought not to be. It doesn't fit in. It is out of relation. It does not please. Then I may come to *acceptance*. I do not see how it fits in to the whole creative process of art, but I have become sufficiently aware of the "sinfulness" of my evaluations . . . that in humility I accept it. It is the work of a good creator who desires it, though I do not desire or understand it. This may be followed by affirmation. It ought to be. It ought to be recognized, affirmed, hung in galleries. But my response is not yet response to the creator until I understand it, contemplate, study it, find out what is in the mind of the artist.

Finally the attitude means cultivation of the created realities about one. "This expresses itself in an education which genuinely 'educes' what God put into the creature, in an art which is discovery and communication of meanings of the form of things, in a science which . . . seeks to think the thoughts of God after him, in a political life which undertakes to realize the created essence of a community."[44]

In sum, this newly won attitude means that Christians

> can accept their relativities with faith in the infinite Absolute to whom all their relative views, values and duties are subject. In the last case they can make their confessions and decisions both with confidence and with the humility which accepts completion and correction and even conflict from and with others who stand in the same relation to the Absolute. They will then in their fragmentary knowledge be able to state with conviction what they have seen and heard, the truth for them; but they will not contend that it is the whole truth and nothing but the truth, and they will not become dogmatists unwilling to seek out what other men have seen and heard of that same object they have fragmentarily known. . . . Just because faith knows of such an absolute standpoint it can therefore accept the relativity of the believer's situation and knowledge.[45]

2. THE IDENTIFICATION OF BEING AND VALUE IN GOD

Niebuhr seeks the ultimate reconciliation of being and value in his conception of God. He expresses this in *Radical Monotheism and Western Culture* by claiming that "monotheism is less than radical if it makes a distinction between the principle of being and the principle of value":

> Radical monotheism is not in the first instance a theory about being and then a faith, as though the faith orientation toward the principle of being as value-center needed to be preceded by an ontology that established the unity of the realm of being and its source in a single power beyond it. It is not at all evident that the One beyond the many, whether made known in revelation or always present to man in hiddenness, is

114

principle of being before it is principle of value. Believing man does not say first, "I believe in a creative principle," and then, "I believe that the principle is gracious, that is, good toward what issues from it." He rather says, "I believe in God the Father, Almighty Maker of heaven and earth." This is a primary statement, a point of departure and not a deduction. In it the principle of being is identified with the principle of value and the principle of value with the principle of being.[46]

This identification is expressed more existentially as the reconciliation of goodness and power in God. Niebuhr speaks of "the two great problems of existence":

The first of these is the problem of the goodness of Power. The great anxiety of life, the great distrust, appears in the doubt that the Power whence all things come, the Power which has thrown the self and its companions into existence, is not good. The question is always before us, Is Power good? Is it good to and for what it has brought into Being? Is it good with the goodness of integrity? Is it good as adorable and delightful? On the other hand we know something of what true goodness is. We recognize goodness in that which maintains and serves being. We recognize the presence of goodness in every form of loyalty and love. But our great question is whether goodness is powerful, whether it is not forever defeated in actual existence by loveless, thoughtless power.[47]

Whatever his stated intentions are, Niebuhr fails in his own discussion of God to make the desired identification between being and value and instead consistently subordinates the principle of value to the principle of being, and God's goodness to God's power.[48]

Niebuhr's claim that God is not first known as principle of

being, then as principle of value, is striking when viewed in relation to Niebuhr's understanding of the movement from distrust of being to trust. His view of that movement, as we saw in the previous section, hinges on the believer's transvaluation of that being, that total context, up against which believers finds themselves. In revelation the believer does not come to know a being that was before unknown; for "the content of revelation is not the self-disclosure of an unknown being, but the unveiling of the value of a known being."[49] Niebuhr uses this point to criticize Tillich's *Systematic Theology*: "The problem of ultimate concern to many men does not seem stateable simply in terms of being but only of being and value; they know of the ground of being, but what they do not know is the goodness of that ground."[50] When Niebuhr describes the movement of faith as being from God the void, to God the enemy, to God the companion[51] the implication is again that God is known first as principle of being and then only later as the principle of value. In the power/goodness terminology Niebuhr expresses this matter by saying that the "alien and inscrutable power that elects us and all things into existence" comes to be known as "the One creative power" in the response of faith.[52] In all these various formulations the point seems clear: we do first come to know God as principle of being.

A possible interpretation is that these passages show being to be epistemologically, not ontologically, prior to value. That we first come to know God's being before we learn of God's value does not mean that in God, God's being *is* subordinate to God's value. Two points might be raised against this interpretation. First, in the crucial passage in *Radical Monotheism* in which Niebuhr talks of the identification of the principle of being with the principle of value, his point is that the identification is epistemological. "Believing man," he says, "does not first say, 'I believe in a creative principle,' and then, 'I believe that the principle is gracious, is good toward what issues from it.'" Rather in human knowing, that identification is "a primary statement, a point of departure."[53] Thus, he says that neither principle is epistemologically primary, though a careful analysis of his discussion of the movement from distrust to trust shows being to be epistemologically prior.

But this is an answer to only a minor point. The main point of the interpretation must still be met: the epistemological primacy of being in his discussion of faith in God does not by itself entail that being is ontologically primary. Though not entailed, the ontological primacy of being can be shown in Niebuhr's view of God.

Niebuhr aptly describes the fundamental conviction underlying the development of his thought as that of God's sovereignty.[54] But that sovereignty is expressed more often with images relating to the sovereignty of God's being or of God's power rather than God's goodness. Indeed, images of God's power are more pervasive in Niebuhr's thought than are images of God's will, the more traditional image associated with sovereignty.

In Niebuhr's early works, the image of structure is used to speak of God's sovereignty. One of Niebuhr's most succinct statements of his view of God is found in a 1932 contribution to *The Christian Century:*

God, I believe, is always in history; he is the structure in things, the source of all meaning, the "I am that I am," that which is that it is. He is the rock against which we beat in vain, that which bruises and overwhelms us when we seek to impose our wishes, contrary to his, upon him. That structure of the universe, that creative will, can no more be said to interfere brutally in history than the violated laws of my organism can be said to interfere brutally with my life if they make me pay the cost of my violation. That structure of the universe, that will of God, does bring war and depression upon us when we bring it on ourselves, for we live in the kind of world which visits our iniquities upon us and our children, no matter how much we pray and desire that it be otherwise.[55]

The images of structure in this passage are notable. God is described as "the structure of things," "the rock against which we beat in vain," "that which bruises and overwhelms us," and "that structure of the universe." These images become determinative for the two uses of "will"; God's will is the structure of the universe. Images of will as personal intention are not to be found.

Another central passage for understanding Niebuhr's view of God employs the image of God as "the way things are":

What is it that is responsible for this passing, that dooms our human faith to frustration? We may call it the nature of things, we may call it fate, we may call it reality. But by whatever name we call it, this law of things, this reality, this way things are, is something with which we all must reckon. We may not be able to give a name to it, calling it only the "void" out of which everything comes and to which everything returns, though that is also a name. But it is there—the last shadowy and vague reality, the secret of existence by virtue of which things come into being, are what they are, and pass away. Against it there is no defense. This reality, this nature of things, abides when all else passes. It is the source of all things and the end of all. It surrounds our life as the great abyss into which all things plunge and as the great source whence they all come. What it is we do not know save that it is and that it is the supreme reality with which we must reckon.[56]

Again, strong images of being predominate. This reality which Christians learn to call God is called "the nature of things," "the law of things," "the last shadowy and vague reality," and "the source of all things and the end of all." And again the human is depicted as helpless in the face of the utter being of that which confronts it: "Against it there is no defense." God for Niebuhr is the structure in things, the reality against which human life is played out.

In the contexts in which they occur the above passages are followed by qualifications of the structure/being imagery, qualifications that arise from seeing the structure of things through the interpretive patterns of faith. Niebuhr qualifies the first passage by saying: "But this same structure in things which is our enemy is our redeemer; 'it means intensely and means good'—not the good which we desire, but the good which we would desire if we were really good and really wise."[57] Nevertheless, the valuational interpretation that is given in faith does not change the ontic experience of the structure. It is not that we come to see that our perception of the reality and structure of being prior to faith was wrong. Nor is it that we come to see that our natural valuation of that structure as inimical to human existence was wrong.[58] Rather, through faith we come to see that structure differently; we come to view it as friendly, as ultimately supportive, not of Christian life, nor human life, nor even life itself alone, but of all being. Insofar as it is supportive of the last-mentioned, that structure may well still be destructive of the aforementioned. This point can be seen in the qualification that follows the second passage cited above:

To attach faith, hope, and love to this last being, this source of all things and this slayer of all, is to have confidence which is not subject to time, for this is the eternal reality, this is the last power. It is to have a love for that which is not exclusive but inclusive, since this reality, this great X, is the source of all things and the end of all. It is, therefore, to be put into the position of those who can love all things in him or in it, and who deny all things in it. "It is a consoling idea," wrote Kierkegaard, "that before God we are always in the wrong." All the relative judgments of worth are equalized in the presence of this One who loves all and hates all, but whose love like whose hatred is without emotion, without favoritism. To have hope of this One is to have hope that is eternal. This being cannot pass away. And to hope for the manifestations of his judgments and his love is to hope to eternity.[59]

This passage makes clear that we still see that structure up against which we find ourselves, even after we are given the gift of faith, as the great X, as the last being, as the eternal reality. We see the same *objective content*. We come to interpret it no longer as inimical but as good, not good for us as isolated individuals nor as an isolated species, but good for the whole. As humans we are part of being, subject to the structures that underlie and determine all being. To trust in something unassailable is to give ourselves to that which is most universally determinative of those structures of which we find ourselves a part.

Two sentences in the just-quoted passage exemplify a problem that is present in less explicit ways in much of Niebuhr's thought. The problem centers in the ideas that we can love all things or deny all things in God, and that God is the One who loves all and hates all. Love and hate are usually descriptive of conflicting dispositions. One may certainly love or hate something; and of two people, one may hate the same thing that the other loves. But we rarely use the two terms in conjunction because the dispositions to which they refer are opposite and contrasting, and hence incompatible.[60] However, when they are used in conjunction, as they are by Niebuhr, the connotation is that of indifference. If God hates all and loves all equally, what is to distinguish God's hating and loving from merely God's indifference? The implication in this passage is that there is very little.

This points to a larger problem: value language has its proper home only where there is an implicit or explicit comparison. If I call something good, then I must have in mind what that something would be if it were bad, or at least less good. To say that it is good is to say that on a scale from best to worst, it is on the whole better than that to which it is being compared. To make such a judgment may be to compare actual existents. For example, if I say, "This is a good razor," I could be comparing it to the last razor I had. More often, however, it is to compare an existent thing or being to some ideal in my mind; a "good" razor is one that favorably compares to the functional idea of an ideal razor—i.e., a razor that shaves closely, smoothly, easily, without nicking, lasts a long time, etc. If the context of a statement does not imply a comparative judgment, then we do not use value language. If I were shaving and someone asked me what was in my hand, I would simply reply, "It's my razor," because there is no comparative implication in the context. If I were to answer, "It's my good razor," an implicit comparative context becomes presupposed; the connotation is that, of my two (or more) razors, the one that is in my hand is the good one, the one better than the other(s).

When Niebuhr identifies being and value in God, a comparative context is made impossible. If whatever is, is good, then nothing can be bad for God. Anything, insofar as it has being, must be good because of its being, its existence. If something were bad, however, it would still be, still exist. Yet in Niebuhr's view, if something is, it is good for God. Therefore nothing can be bad for God.

The oddity of this argument rests on the difficulty of the identification of being and value. In common language the attribution of existence to a thing is distinguished from the attribution of value. To say that something exists is not at all to say that it is good or that it is bad, for as I argued above, value terms are applicable only in situations of comparison between or among beings. Yet for God there can be no comparative distinction among beings; God "loves all and hates all . . . without favoritism." "Good" when applied to beings from the divine perspective has therefore to mean something rather different from what it means in our ordinary usage.

That "good" has a different meaning when used to speak of the good-for-God can be seen in the difficulty Niebuhr has relating the good-for-God to his definition of the good as the fitting. We have seen that he defines the good relationally as "that which meets the needs, which fits the capacity, which corresponds to the potentialities of an existent being."[61] His structural view of value depends on the objective needs beings have for other beings, so that a being can be said to be good for another only insofar as it fits the other's needs. But the Absolute can have no needs. On Niebuhr's view God cannot need created being because God would then not be absolute.[62] Niebuhr recognizes this dilemma and suggests a possible escape:

> [Radical monotheism's] starting point, its dogmatic beginning, is with the transcendent One for whom alone there is an ultimate good and for whom, as the source and end of all things, whatever is, is good. It may indeed use a sort of psychological relativism at this point, since it cannot say that God has need of any being external to himself; hence it may be able only to say that whatever is exists because it pleases God. But whether the relation is to need or to desire, in any case the starting point is that transcendent absolute for whom, or for which, whatever is, is good.[63]

His attempt to refer to desire rather than needs when thinking of the good-for-God is puzzling, to say the least. He rejects, as we have seen, that value can be defined in terms of desires, for that would be to subjectivize it. And this would then mean "that there is nothing good or ill but thinking makes it so."[64] Yet he appeals to the fact of God's desires to make intelligible what it might mean to talk about the good-for-God. *That is, he defines the good-for-God in precisely those terms which he rejects as inadequate for the definition of the value of anything else.* Having defined the good-for-God in terms of desire, would Niebuhr be willing to say that "there is nothing good or ill for God but thinking makes it so?" Probably not, because this would mean that one could distinguish between a thing's being and God's valuing of it. And that, as we have seen, Niebuhr wants to deny. The phrase could be made consistent with his view if one merely dropped a few words and changed another so that the phrase would instead read "there is nothing but God's being makes so." Indeed, this revised version would not be a bad summary statement of the whole of Niebuhr's thought.

If in Niebuhr's earlier works the image of structure is associated with God's being, in his later works the image of power is more often used. In the fourth chapter of *The Responsible Self* Niebuhr uses the image of power to describe the self's experience of being absolutely dependent. He suggests that the religious element in our lives as selves arises out of the inexplicable contingency of our existence. Why certain aspects of our life are the way they are, aspects like our biological characteristics and our ideas and ways of thinking, can be explained. Biological characteristics are the result of genetic factors enclosed deep within cellular structures, and ideas and ways of thinking can be traced to sociohistorical contexts. But two features of our existence are inexplicable and remain uninterpreted: "the radical action by which I was cast into this particular historical . . . process, so that my interpretations and responses are directed toward particular challenges . . . ; and the action by which I am."[65] For Niebuhr, one can only understand our inexplicable contingency by referring it, not to any of the finite powers by which we understand most other aspects of our existence, but to "the alien and inscrutable power that elects us and all things into existence."[66] The religious problem comes to be described as the problem of "trust and distrust in the ultimate power of being."[67]

The basic thrust of these images of power in Niebuhr's thought is similar to that of the images of structure: it points to the fundamentality of God's being. We come to interpret the "alien and inscrutable power" as friendly, but the basic ontic character of that power is not thereby changed. Our view of God may be changed; we may see God in a way that we had not before. Nevertheless God's being remains that same power that confronts us whether we interpret it in trust or in distrust.

Because of its strong emphasis on the sovereignty of God's being, Niebuhr's thought is nearly deterministic and fatalistic. He speaks several times of God as "the Determiner of Destiny."[68] In the imagery of structure, God is said to be "the structure of things to which we must conform unless we are willing to be damned together."[69] And Niebuhr observes that "the actual structure of things is such that our wishes for a different result do not in the least affect the outcome. . . . This God of things as they are is inevitable and quite merciless."[70] History is therefore not "an indeterminate sequence of events where men may adjust themselves to a relatively stable environment and to each other, but [is] a driving, directional movement ruthless so far as individuals and nations are concerned, almost impersonal in its determinism."[71]

A deterministic strain can also be seen when Niebuhr employs the imagery of power:

> How free are we? We become aware that we are much less free than we thought. Our lives are more determined than we like to think. We did not come into existence by our own power, nor do we pass out of it by our own power. Therefore the last and greatest freedom is for our lives: we must consent to live. We can, it is true, take our physical life; we can exercise the freedom to die—we can commit suicide. But, if the Creator has made us so that we continue to exist after our biological death, it is not in our power to die. Even in suicide we do not have the power to decide for or against life itself; whether we live on after our biological death is not

124

under our control. We are in the hands of God, under a divine determinism, and there is nothing we can do about it if our spiritual life goes on.[72]

Yet Niebuhr distinguishes his view of determinism from divine foreordination. The latter interprets divine determinism according to the symbols of teleology. "When this One [this determining power] is understood, with the use of the symbols of making and of design, as the predesigner, the foreordainer of all that happens, then indeed, nothing but fatalism could result from an ethics of response to God." In contrast, Niebuhr argues that his symbolism of responsibility allows for human freedom, for it is built on the metaphor of dialogue rather than of machines. God's relation to the world is hence better conceived through the images of the kingdom and the family:

> The [images] of the kingdom and of the family are, to be sure, symbols also, but they do greater justice to our actual experience of life. They fit this dialogue in which our free acts take place in response to actions over which we have no power, in which our free acts are not truly *ours*, and free, unless they are the consequences of interpretation. They fit the dialogue also in which our free actions can never be freed from the responses that will be made to them. Our freedom presupposes and anticipates action not subject to our control. To think of the determination to which we are so subject as in itself invariant after the manner of a machine is to become enslaved by an erroneous myth.[73]

What is at stake here is conceiving of the power that acts on us as personal. We have no freedom over the ultimate alteraction that confronts us; nor do we have control over the reaction to our action. Our freedom is limited to the way we interpret the alteraction, and that interpretation will determine our response. But the crucial question is: Will our action in response to the divine action itself become an alter-action for God? Niebuhr defines action as being responsive to alteration. If we then talk of God's action, do we similarly mean that it is responsive?

Niebuhr is ambiguous on this point. On the one hand, he does indicate that our actions are responded to by God. In speaking of Jesus' interpretation of God's action Niebuhr writes:

> The will of God is what God does in all that nature and men do. It is the universal that contains and transforms, includes and fashions, every particular. . . . [Jesus'] interpretation of every alteration as included in, or as taken up by, the action of God was neither fatalistic nor mechanical. The idea that all acts of finite agents had been predesigned, as though God were the author of a play in which each actor played a predestined role, is remote from Jesus' way of thinking. The Universal One whom he calls Father is Lord of heaven and earth. His action is more like that of the great wise leader who uses even the meannesses of his subjects to promote the public welfare.[74]

On the other hand, the images that we have above examined—images of God as the structure in things, as the Determiner of Destiny, and as the alien and inscrutable power that elects us and all things into existence—picture a much less responsive being than do those of king and father. And I think it is fair to say in general that one more often finds in Niebuhr's work images of power and structure than images of king and father. [75]

CHAPTER SEVEN

Conclusion

W E MUST TAKE stock of the results of our study. We began by looking at Niebuhr's theory of value as a philosophical proposal. We saw that his theory could indeed be approached from this perspective because in "The Center of Value" he himself attempts such an analysis. Fundamental to his theory is the thoroughly relative character of value. Value is attributable to a being only in regard to some other being, so that "X is good" must be stated in a way that clarifies the relation in which X is good; that is, it must be stated in the form "X is good for Y." Nothing is good in and of itself but only in its relations.

Yet Niebuhr avoids the subjectivist implications of such a relativistic approach to value by defining value relations in terms of needs. These needs are structurally objective in that they are properties of relations between beings and can be defined in terms of fittingness. What is good for a being is what fits that being's needs, not what that being desires, wants, or even thinks fits its needs.

Niebuhr introduces the idea of "god" into his discussion of value theory in order to describe how persons make value decisions in the face of the relational relativity of value. Since value can be predicated only in a relation, it is possible for a being to be good for one being and yet bad for another. Yet value judgments must be made in life. Niebuhr suggests that what actually happens in such decisions is that one value relation is taken as definitive for decision. Whether something is good, is determined by whether it is good for some being, taken as a center of value. For patriots, whether or not something is to be chosen depends on whether it is good for their country; for egotists, whether it is good for themselves; for humanists, whether it is good for humanity. In each of these cases some one relation is taken as definitive for decision, though which relation is so taken is dogmatically relative. Since choosing such a center of value always involves choosing some one being for whom the good is finally judged to be good, Niebuhr suggests that these centers of value are properly termed "gods."

Up to this point, Niebuhr intends his theory as a description of value and the situations in which we make decisions among values. Many value theories are developed primarily to provide normative criteria for making judgments. But Niebuhr's theory is not best understood in this way; indeed it cannot be. For the description of value which he gives shows value to be relative to a center which is dogmatically accepted as the starting point for decision and judgment. What his theory shows is that all our values are relative to our various value centers. To think that our values are absolute, good apart from beings for whom they are good, is to misunderstand the nature of value.

To see the real function of Niebuhr's value theory within his thought as a whole, we might ask a question that Niebuhr would find most congenial: To whom was he responding? What was the alteraction that gave rise to his value theory? The answer is that he was responding to the liberals' use of value considerations in their theology. Two things especially trouble Niebuhr about the way liberals deal with values. First of all, he is unhappy with the fact that "they assume that men have a knowledge of absolutely valid values which is not only independent of their knowledge of God but which is also in some way determinative of God."[1] Secondly, he is troubled by the way that the liberals tend to separate values from being, so that they are prejudiced "for the goodness of the spiritual as opposed to the material, and for the goodness of the nonexistent as opposed to the existent."[2] It is as a reaction to these two factors, rather than as a theory of comparative value, that Niebuhr's theory must be seen. In his thought as a whole, Niebuhr's value theory serves the function of pointing out that "none is absolute save God and that the absolutizing of anything finite is ruinous to the finite itself."[3]

But Niebuhr also comes at the issue of value from a wholly different direction. He not only works at the problem of value from the theoretical side, but also from the religious or theological side. The experience of being valued by God is for Niebuhr, "primitive and original."[4] That fundamental experience makes possible for Niebuhr that trust or distrust in Being that is definitive of faith. If a center of value is, in his value theory, that being in relation to which good is judged to be good and evil, evil, then in his understanding of faith, the center of value is that which is the source of the self's value, that which actually values the self.

The connection between the theoretical and theological movements is found in the affirmation, whatever is, is good. In Niebuhr's theory of value that affirmation amounts to the critical principle that no relative values are good in the sense that absolute values are good for God. Yet in his theology of value that affirmation functions more positively to inform the whole life attitude of the self who has been valued by God. Knowing that whatever is, is ultimately valued by God means that we take a new attitude toward all relative values. They are still relative, and conflict and competition among them are an inevitable part of our finite existence. But the attitude with which we approach those values will be one of acceptance and affirmation. Behind all the relativities of life, all the transient values that face us in our daily existence, stands God the Center of Value—the One for whom whatever is, is good.

Recognizing that there is a double movement in Niebuhr's discussion helps us understand why it was difficult to examine the theoretical movement detached from the theological. The problem we encountered was how Niebuhr's theory of value could be considered "an aid to accuracy of action" and contribute to better value decisions, given the overwhelmingly critical role that it seemed to play. But the analysis has shown that it provides such aid by defining the appropriate attitude with which to make relative decisions. Hence the difficulty is partially resolved when his value theory is viewed in its proper context, as integrally related to his theology of value.

But this does not explain the problem Niebuhr has trying to hold together in God the principle of being and the principle of value. Being and value have always been important in Judeo-Christian conceptions of God. Niebuhr wants to claim that the principle of being and the principle of value are one in God. Yet, Niebuhr is able to hold these two principles together only by subsuming the principle of value to the principle of being. And in his value theory itself, value reduces to being, in that it is defined in terms of structural relations between beings.

The problem here may well stem from Niebuhr's attempt to focus on God primarily as the One. His discussion of radical monotheism may be construed as an effort to think through the implications of a radically monotheistic view of reality. In such a view, unity becomes a crucial determination for conceiving the ultimate context of human existence. But the One that stands beyond the many must for Niebuhr be an inclusive one, for otherwise the manyness would not be ultimately taken up by the unity, but would stand over against it. Unity hence becomes for Niebuhr primarily a unity of being, the unity of the One Being that stands behind the many finite beings.

The question might be raised whether the unity fundamental in a religious conception of God is a unity of goodness rather than being. What is sought after in religion is not so much the one being behind the many but the one good being that is worthy of devotion, trust, and loyalty. Whether that being be envisioned as the One inclusive being, the One transcendent being, or even one being among the many, is less important than that it be the being worthy of our trust and loyalty. Niebuhr himself seems at points to recognize this, for he sees that "whatever else deity may be in philosophical definition or practical worship it must be value."[5] But he goes on to say that the deity's value must always be balanced by the deity's being, or as he often says, by the deity's power: "Deity, whatever else it must be to be deity, must be powerful in its goodness as well as good in its power."[6] Yet his attempt to ascribe both ultimate power and ultimate goodness to God ends up not balancing but subsuming goodness to power and value to being.

John Cobb convincingly argues that being and value are not ultimately reconcilable. He speaks of the principle of being as metaphysical ultimateness and the principle of value as the ultimate of rightness and, tracing the development of the Judeo-Christian idea of God in the West, shows that "there have been efforts to assimilate the metaphysical ultimate to the ultimate of rightness, but the resultant syntheses have proved unstable." In the face of this instability he suggests that "it is best to reaffirm [God's] identification with the principle of rightness; for worship is directed to this."[7] Cobb's own interest in making the distinction arises out of the Whiteheadian perspective in which he works. But Cobb's point can be made another way, a way growing out of Niebuhr's own thought.

In our relations of trust and loyalty with each other as persons, the other's goodness and not their power fundamentally shapes our faith in them. When I trust another, I trust that they will always act toward me with good intentions, that they will do what they can for me in whatever circumstances we find ourselves together. If, for instance, I find myself trapped in an automobile after an accident and a trusted companion is unhurt and able to help me, my trust in that companion is that they will do whatever they can to free me. My companion may try to free me by brute force, but if my companion is frail such efforts may be to no avail. But then my companion can go for help and find someone who is strong enough to extricate me from the wreck.

But what if my companion, too, is injured. It might then be that they are unable either to extricate me from the wreck themselves or to go for help in time to save my life. Indeed they may be powerless to do anything in the situation. Does this mean that my trust in them was disappointed, that they were faithless to me? Of course not. For my trust in a companion is not predicated on whether or not they have the power to do anything for me in the situation, but on the constancy of their good intentions toward me.

Of course, issues of power are also involved in such trusting relationships. There is a sense, for example, that the trust I have in physicians implicitly refers to the powers that they have to heal. My trust, however, is not predicated on those powers but on their good intentions toward me. It may be that I come to have a terminal illness in face of which my physicians are powerless. But I can still trust them if they keep faith with me, letting me know that they are powerless. On the other hand, more skillful, powerful healers might be found in a research institution; they might have new experimental procedures to test that might prove powerful against my disease. Yet if I sense their intentions toward me are less determinative for their actions than their research goals, if I fear that they carry out the experimental trials primarily for the good of research and not for my good, then all the power they have is not enough to create that trust in and loyalty to them that is so decisive for my faith in them.

If goodness and not power is fundamental in relations of human trusting, and if we use, as does Niebuhr, the image of trusting relationships as a root metaphor for understanding faith in God, why should not God's goodness be more fundamental than God's power in our conception of God? Whatever the case philosophically, it is enough religiously to trust in something that we perceive to be fundamentally good whether or not it has all the power that is.

Niebuhr's attempt to reconcile goodness and power, value and being, ends by subordinating one to the other. If an identification of being and value is impossible and a reconciliation of the two always results in subordination, then religiously it is better to make value rather than being, primary.

Notes

CHAPTER 1

1. Thomas Aquinas, *Summa Theologica: First Complete American Edition in Three Volumes*, trans. Fathers of the English Dominican Province (New York: Benziger Bros., 1947–48), 1:23–28 (I*a*, Q.5).

CHAPTER 2

1. H. Richard Niebuhr, "Value-Theory and Theology," in *The Nature of Religious Experience: Essays in Honor of Douglas Clyde Macintosh*, ed. Eugene Garrett Bewkes et al. (New York: Harper & Bros., 1937), pp. 93–116.

These manuscript chapters are in the possession of Richard R. Niebuhr, who kindly gave me access to them. H. Richard Niebuhr's projected title for his *magnum opus* was "The Responsible Self." Since drafts of but two chapters had been written at the time of his death, the decision was made to publish the completed text of the Robertson Lectures, which he delivered under the same title at the University of Glasgow in 1960. These lectures appeared in 1963 as *The Responsible Self: An Essay in Christian Moral Philosophy*. (See Richard R. Niebuhr, Preface to *The Responsible Self* [New York: Harper & Row, 1963], p. 3.) The two draft chapters are considerably expanded versions of the material found in the Robertson Lectures and contain important discussions related to value unavailable elsewhere. Hence in the following I shall refer to these manuscript chapters as "The Responsible Self" manuscript so as to avoid confusion with the published Robertson Lectures of the same title.

2. Bibliographies from Niebuhr's courses in Christian ethics as well as his extant lecture notes show him to have been in dialogue with the work of such philosophical figures as John Dewey, Nikolai

Hartmann, W. D. Ross, A. N. Whitehead, Paul Weiss, and A. J. Ayer. In the opening paragraphs of his essay "The Center of Value" Niebuhr identifies eight philosophers as dialogue partners in his quest to develop a relational theory of value: Plato, Nikolai Hartmann, G. E. Moore, David Hume, Jeremy Bentham, Edward Westermarck, Moritz Schlick, and A. J. Ayer. See "The Center of Value," in *Radical Monotheism and Western Culture: With Supplementary Essays* (New York: Harper & Row, Harper Torchbooks, 1970), pp. 100–101.

3. James M. Gustafson, Foreword to *The Theology of H. Richard Niebuhr*, by Libertus A. Hoedemaker (Philadelphia: Pilgrim Press, 1970), p. ix.

4. H. Richard Niebuhr, *The Meaning of Revelation* (New York: Macmillan Publishing, Macmillan Paperbacks, 1960), p. 29.

5. H. Richard Niebuhr, "Reformation: Continuing Imperative," *Christian Century* 77 (March 1960):250.

6. *The Oxford Dictionary of the Christian Church*, ed. F. L. Cross (London: Oxford University Press, 1958), s.v. "Confessing Church."

7. Karl Barth, *Church Dogmatics*, vol. 1, pt. 2, *The Doctrine of the Word of God*, ed. G. W. Bromiley and T. F. Torrance, trans. G. T. Thomson and Harold Knight (Edinburgh: T. & T. Clark, 1956), p. 828.

8. Niebuhr even explicitly rejects a denominational view of confessionalism: "We have found ourselves in our denominations and confessions debtors to one another, dependent on each other to such a degree that the confessionalist vision is no longer possible, however great our appreciation is of the value of the particular family to which we belong." H. Richard Niebuhr, "The Gift of the Catholic Vision," *Theology Today* 4 (1948):512–13.

9. Though Niebuhr retains throughout the rest of his works the basic epistemological stance and the basic understanding of theology that he develops in *The Meaning of Revelation*, he rarely again refers to his own work as "confessional" theology—a fact which is all the more interesting given his continued propensity to view himself as primarily concerned in his work with the reformation of the church. Even in those books and articles in which he explicitly addresses the issue of theology, he does not again discuss it under the term "confessional." See, for example, "Theology—Not Queen but Servant," *Journal of Religion* 35 (January 1955): 1–5; and *The Purpose of the Church and Its Ministry: Reflections on the Aims of Theological Education* (New York: Harper & Row, Harper's Ministers Paperback Library, 1977).

10. Ph.D. dissertation, Yale University, 1924. (Ann Arbor, Michigan: University Microfilms International, 1965).

11. H. Richard Niebuhr, *The Social Sources of Denominationalism* (New York: The New American Library, Meridian Books, 1975), p. 16.

12. For a summary statement of his conclusion, see *The Kingdom of God in America* (New York: Harper & Row, Harper Torchbooks, 1958), pp. 164–65.

13. Ibid., p. 2. Emphasis added.

14. *The Meaning of Revelation*, p. ix. For a succinct discussion of Tillich's concept of "beliefful realism" see Paul Tillich, *The Protestant Era*, abridged ed., trans. James Luther Adams (Chicago: University of Chicago Press, Phoenix Books, 1957), pp. 62–82. Those pages contain Tillich's revision of a translation of his essay "Ueber glaübiger Realismus," originally published in Tillich's *Religiöse Verwirklichung*, 2te Auflage (Berlin: Furche, 1930), pp. 65–87. For that revised translation Tillich proposed to use the term "self-transcending realism" instead of "belief-ful realism" to render "glaübiger Realismus." See James Luther Adams, *Paul Tillich's Philosophy of Culture, Science, and Religion* (New York: Schocken Books, Schocken Paperbacks, 1970), p. 198, n. 21.

15. *Immanuel Kant's Critique of Pure Reason*, unabridged ed., trans. Norman Kemp Smith (New York: St. Martin's Press, 1965), pp. 71, 82 (B42/A26, B59/A42). Emphasis added.

16. Niebuhr, *The Meaning of Revelation*, p. 7. Cf. *The Responsible Self*, p. 161: "[Man] is a being who grasps and shapes reality, including the actuality of his own existence, with the aid of great images, metaphors, and analogies. These are partly in his conscious mind but so largely in his unconscious mind and in the social language that he tends to take them for granted as forms of pure reason. They are, indeed, forms of reason, but of historic reason."

17. Niebuhr, *The Responsible Self*, p. 96.

18. Niebuhr, *The Meaning of Revelation*, p. 44.

19. Ibid., p. 70.

20. Ibid., pp. 70–71.

21. All quotations in this paragraph are from *The Meaning of Revelation*, p. 71.

22. Ibid., p. 72.

23. Ibid., pp. 79–80.

24. Ibid., p. 73.

25. Ibid., p. 75.

26. See Gilbert Ryle, *The Concept of Mind* (New York: Barnes & Noble, 1949), pp. 16–18. Ryle's use of the concept of category-mistake is limited to misapplications of concepts in a language, a use more limited than what Niebuhr has in mind here with evil imaginations. Nevertheless, Ryle's concept can be used in interpreting Niebuhr, for both Ryle and Niebuhr are concerned to show that using concepts (for Ryle) or images (for Niebuhr) where they are not applicable results in mistakes and confusions (a point which, of course, is reminiscent of Kant's discussion of transcendental dialectic in his *Critique of Pure Reason*).

27. Niebuhr, *The Meaning of Revelation*, p. 80.

28. Niebuhr, "Theological Frontiers," The Cole Lectures, Vanderbilt University, 1960 (transcription from tape recording), lecture 3, p. 7. (Niebuhr manuscript collection.)

29. Ibid., p. 28.

30. Kant, *Critique of Pure Reason*, p. 65 (A19/B33).

31. Ibid., p. 303 (A302/B359).

32. Ibid., p. 533 (A644/B672).

33. Immanuel Kant, *Critique of Practical Reason*, trans. Lewis White Beck, The Library of Liberal Arts (Indianapolis: Bobbs-Merrill, 1956), p. 127.

34. Ibid., p. 30.

35. Niebuhr, *The Purpose of the Church and Its Ministry*, p. 20.

36. Niebuhr, *The Responsible Self*, p. 42.

37. Ibid., pp. 45–46.

38. Ibid., p. 112.

39. Donald E. Fadner in his *Responsible God: A Study of the Christian Philosophy of H. Richard Niebuhr* (American Academy of Religion Dissertation Series, no. 13 [Missoula, Montana: Scholars Press, 1975]) fails to draw this distinction. According to Fadner, Niebuhr thinks the Christian philosopher is able "to render intelligible in a comprehensive way our common human experience" (p. 51). As excellent as much of Fadner's analysis is, it errs on the side of seeing in Niebuhr that which Niebuhr himself criticized in many philosophers—the attempt to set forth a view of human being that ignores the relativity of the various socio-historical contexts in which human beings are always found.

40. See Niebuhr, "Faith on Earth" (Niebuhr manuscript collection), especially chapters 1 and 3: "Faith in Question" and "The Structure of Faith." James W. Fowler has an extensive synopsis of this piece in his *To See the Kingdom: The Theological Vision of H. Richard Niebuhr* (Nashville: Abingdon Press, 1974), pp. 201–247. For a more extensive discussion of Niebuhr's view of faith, see below, chap. 6.

41. H. Richard Niebuhr, "On the Nature of Faith," in *Religious Experience and Truth: A Symposium*, ed. Sidney Hook (New York: New York University Press, 1961), p. 102.

CHAPTER 3

1. Niebuhr, as quoted by James M. Gustafson in his Introduction to *The Responsible Self*, p. 16.

2. H. Richard Niebuhr, "The Alliance between Labor and Religion," *Magazin für evangelische Theologie und Kirche* 49 (1921):203.

3. H. Richard Niebuhr, "Christianity and the Social Problem," *Magazin für evangelische Theologie und Kirche* 50 (1922):290, 291.

4. H. Richard Niebuhr, "The Grace of Doing Nothing," *Christian Century* 49 (1932):379.

5. H. Richard Niebuhr, "War as Crucifixion," *Christian Century* 60 (1943):513.

6. H. Richard Niebuhr, "War as the Judgment of God," *Christian Century* 59 (1942):632.

7. Niebuhr, "War as Crucifixion," p. 515.

8. This tendency to focus on attitudes rather than actions was also characteristic of Niebuhr's approach in his Christian Ethics lectures at Yale Divinity School. Syllabi from various years indicate that Niebuhr typically addressed three special problems during the course of his lectures—responsibility in sex and family life, in the economic community, and in political communities. Regrettably, a section on special problems was not included in his lectures of 1961, the only year for which there exists his own complete notes. A very careful student transcription of his lectures in 1952 exists among his manuscript materials, however, and the section on special problems is included in it. See, Niebuhr, Christian Ethics Lectures, Winter and Spring, 1952 (transcribed by Robert Yetter, Gene Canestrari, and Ed Elliot). Hereafter referred to as the Yetter transcription.

9. See H. Richard Niebuhr, "The Triad of Faith," *Andover Newton Bulletin* 47 (October 1954):3–12. See also his "Faith on Earth," especially chapter 3, "The Structure of Faith."

10. Niebuhr, *The Responsible Self*, p. 71.

11. Niebuhr, Christian Ethics Lectures, 1952 (Yetter transcription), 4 January 1952, p. 1.

12. Ibid., 7 January 1952, p. 4.

13. The individualistic character of Niebuhr's view of the self is also expressed in the following passage on faith: "The immediacy of the self's relation to the power by which it is cannot be supplanted by the mediation of any group of believers. Theology and doctrine are always highly social, representing our responses to each other's reports and interpretations of encounter with the ultimate. But faith as trust and distrust is inexpugnably personal. Of the theories I hold about God and man and human history I may say that they constitute 'no faith of my own' but that of the church. But trust and distrust are my very own." Niebuhr, *The Responsible Self*, p. 120.

14. See James Gustafson, "Context Versus Principles: A Misplaced Debate in Christian Ethics," *Harvard Theological Review* 58 (April 1965):185.

15. Niebuhr, *The Responsible Self*, pp. 61, 65.

16. Ibid., p. 126.

17. H. Richard Niebuhr, "The Christian Church in the World's Crisis," *Christianity and Society* 6 (1941):11.

18. Ibid.

19. Ibid.

20. Ibid., p. 12.

21. Ibid.

22. D. M. Yeager ("On Making the Tree Good: An Apology for a Dispositional Ethics," *Journal of Religious Ethics* 10/1 [Spring 1982]: 103–120) also argues that Niebuhr's emphasis rests on the attitudes of the agent rather than the character of specific actions. She attributes this to Niebuhr's being a dispositional ethicist. Dispositional ethicists, she argues, are not interested in principles for moral action or value judgments but in the traits and dispositions that must be cultivated within persons so that they might become

good. Right acts will hence flow out of one who has become good. Yeager dismisses much of the criticism leveled against the lack of concreteness within Niebuhr's normative program because it fails to recognize that Niebuhr is a dispositional ethicist.

Yeager's analysis highlights an important aspect of Niebuhr's thought that has received little attention. She is right to point within Niebuhr's analysis to the pivotal role that one's disposition toward the whole context of one's action plays in shaping the life lived in responsibility. Yet I believe she overplays the significance of disposition within his analysis by classifying Niebuhr's overall position as dispositional, for that too strongly implies that value is to be defined primarily in terms of the self and its virtues. Following this line of interpretation she revealingly concludes that Niebuhr "offers this moral philosophy to us because he believes that it will enable us to approach, as it enabled him to approach, that which we all long to achieve: the happy life" (p. 119). Her eudaemonistic interpretation of Niebuhr is surprising because there is so little evidence that he understood himself in this way. Niebuhr never describes his project in terms of achieving the happy life. Furthermore, in "The Center of Value" he defines value relationally and specifically rejects the notion that the virtues are good in a self apart from the way that they are good in relation to other selves. That is to say, the goods of the self—and here I believe it would be appropriate to include "the happy life"—are secondary, not primary in Niebuhr's relational ethics.

23. Niebuhr employs the term "being" in the broadest of possible senses: "being" refers to something or someone that is, that exists. Persons and animals are beings, but so are plants and inanimate things. Beings do not necessarily have mind or consciousness, a fact important when Niebuhr defines value in terms of needs rather than conscious desires. (See below, chap. 3.)

24. Niebuhr, "The Center of Value," p. 107.

25. Ibid., p. 100.

26. I use "characteristic" here rather than "quality" or "category" to maintain the ambiguity present in Niebuhr's discussion, for he never clearly specifies what sort of thing value is. George Schrader in his analysis and critique of Niebuhr's value theory ("Value and Valuation," in *Faith and Ethics: The Theology of H. Richard Niebuhr*, ed. Paul Ramsey [New York: Harper & Row, Harper Torchbooks, 1965], pp. 173–204) recognizes this and correctly observes that Niebuhr does not so much offer a definition of value in terms of the relation of being to being as he simply tries to indicate "the conditions under which value occurs" (p. 175). Schrader goes on, however, to suggest that value for Niebuhr is a category in the Kantian sense, that Niebuhr "actually considers it to be a category which has no meaning apart from the evaluative subject and the situation within which he judges" (p. 178). To interpret "value" as a category in this sense is to over-subjectivize what Niebuhr intends. He is unwilling to collapse the meaning of value into that of valuation and say that something is valuable means that someone values it. Value for Niebuhr is not subjective in the ontological sense that value would have no existence if there were no conscious valuers.

27. Niebuhr, "The Center of Value," p. 102.

28. R. B. Perry, who like Niebuhr develops a thoroughly relational theory of value, also argues that value is not reducible to the cognitive act of judging value. Both theorists reject the aphorism, "There is nothing either good or bad, but thinking makes it so" (see Niebuhr, "Value-Theory and Theology," p. 106; Perry, *General Theory of Value* [New York: Longmans, Green, & Co., 1926], p. 129). But for Perry value is dependent on "the motor-affective life" of beings who have such lives. Hence it is relative to the "state, act, attitude or disposition of favor or disfavor" (p. 115). Perry's is a more subjective view of value than Niebuhr's, for unless a subject presently has or in the past has had a disposition to have a feeling of favor or disfavor, then value cannot be said to be present.

29. Niebuhr, "The Center of Value," p. 103.

30. Niebuhr, "Value-Theory and Theology," p. 113.

31. Niebuhr, "The Center of Value," pp. 102–3.

32. Niebuhr further defines this objectivity of needs by the idea of "fittingness." See chapter 5 below.

33. Niebuhr, "The Center of Value," p. 103.

34. Schrader, "Value and Valuation," p. 184.

35. In *Moral Principles of Action: Man's Ethical Imperative*, pp. 162–175, ed. Ruth Nanda Anshen, Science of Culture Series, vol. 5 (New York: Harper & Bros., 1952). References to this earlier version will hereafter be cited as "'The Center of Value' (1952)." References to the revised version appearing in *Radical Monotheism* *and Western Culture* (1960) will be given simply as "The Center of Value."

36. Niebuhr, "The Center of Value" (1952), p. 166.

37. Niebuhr, "The Center of Value," p. 105, n. 1.

38. Niebuhr's denial that any being is good in and of itself means that he has difficulty in speaking of God's goodness. See below, chap. 6.

39. Niebuhr, "The Center of Value," p. 106.

40. The term "value systems" follows Niebuhr's own usage (see, for instance, "The Center of Value," p. 112). One must not think, however, that his use of that term is limited only to theoretical applications. Value systems are a real part of everyone's world-view, passed down through the socialization process in which we are nurtured as selves. One can reflect on such systems and theorize about them, but such reflections presuppose that the systems are operative within and among us whether or not they are self-consciously articulated.

41. Donald E. Fadner misses this important point. "The center of value," he argues, "is that being for which all other beings are good but which is not itself good for any other being. Accordingly, the center of value is that being relative to whose subjective good the objective or complementary value of all other beings is determined, but whose subjective good is not itself defined by reference to any other being; the center of value does not 'need' anything beyond itself to define its own subjective good." *The Responsible God*, p. 154.

42. Niebuhr, "The Center of Value," p. 109.

43. Ibid., p. 110.

44. Ibid.

45. Niebuhr, "Value-Theory and Theology," p. 106.

CHAPTER 4

1. Indeed, this is Niebuhr's chief criticism of Ritschlian value-theology. Niebuhr senses that the reduction of faith to mere valuation means that along with it God is reduced to mere ideal or eternal values, and these in turn reflect merely "the value-scale of civilized man" (*The Meaning of Revelation*, p. 21). He makes this point vividly in an unpublished fragment entitled "Faith, Reason, Feeling, Valuing" (Niebuhr manuscript collection): "To believe is not the same as to value anymore than it is the same to think or to feel; however closely the God of faith is related to supreme value or to the universal idea or the numinous he is not to be readily identified with these."

2. Niebuhr, *Radical Monotheism*, p. 16.

3. "The valuation of which man becomes aware in religious experience is not first of all his evaluation of a being, but that being's evaluation of him." Niebuhr, "Value-Theory and Theology," p. 115.

4. Niebuhr, *Radical Monotheism*, p. 17.

5. Ibid., p. 18.

6. Niebuhr, "The Triad of Faith," pp. 7–8. Corrected according to the errata accompanying the article.

7. "A cause is good," says Royce, "not only for me, but for mankind, in so far as it is essentially a *loyalty* to *loyalty*, that is, is an aid and a furtherance of loyalty in my fellows. It is an evil cause in so far as, despite the loyalty that it arouses in me, it is destructive in the world of my fellows." Josiah Royce, *The Philosophy of Loyalty* (New York: Macmillan Co., 1908), pp. 118–19.

8. Niebuhr, "Faith on Earth," chap. 3, p. 22.

9. The synonymity of "cause" and "center of value" can be seen in the following passage: "Centers of value and causes may . . . be only two names for the same objective realities from which and for which selves live as valued and valuing beings." Niebuhr, *Radical Monotheism*, p. 22.

10. For a discussion of the two perspectives, see above, pp. 11–18.

11. Niebuhr, "The Center of Value," p. 109.

12. Niebuhr, "Faith in Gods and in God," in *Radical Monotheism*, p. 118.

13. See Niebuhr, "Life is Worth Living," *Intercollegian and Far Horizons* 57 (October 1939):3–4, 22.

14. Niebuhr, "Faith in Gods and in God," p. 118.

15. Ibid., pp. 117, 118, 119.

16. Niebuhr, *Radical Monotheism*, p. 24.

17. Niebuhr, "The Center of Value," p. 111.

18. Niebuhr, *Radical Monotheism*, p. 24.

19. Niebuhr, "Value-Theory and Theology," p. 114.

20. If there were two or more discrete infinite beings, each would limit the other in that each would exclude the other's being; hence neither would be infinite.

21. Niebuhr, "The Center of Value," p. 112.

22. Ibid., p. 111.

23. Niebuhr, *Radical Monotheism*, p. 25.

24. Niebuhr, "Faith in Gods and in God," p. 120.

25. Ibid., p. 121.

26. "The self as one self among all the systematized reactions in which it engages seems to be the counterpart of a unity that lies beyond, yet expresses itself in, all the manifold systems of actions upon it. In religious language, the soul and God belong together; or otherwise stated, I am one within myself as I encounter the One in all that acts upon me. . . . To respond to the ultimate action in all responses to finite actions means to seek one integrity of self amidst all the integrities of scientific, political, economic, educational, and other cultural activities; it means to be one responding self amidst all the responses of the roles being played, because there is present to the self the One other beyond all the finite systems of nature and society." Niebuhr, *The Responsible Self*, pp. 122–23.

27. David L. Miller in his *New Polytheism: Rebirth of the Gods and Goddesses* (New York: Harper & Row, 1974) takes Niebuhr to task for his radical monotheism. Miller thinks Niebuhr's monotheistic thinking, like all monotheistic thinking, is "abstract, dogmatic, doctrinal, and creedal" (p. 28). In contrast he suggests that "the multiple patterns of polytheism allow room to move meaningfully through a pluralistic universe. They free one to affirm the radical plurality of the self, an affirmation that one has seldom been able to manage because of the guilt of monotheism's insidious implication that we have to 'get it all together.' . . . What a relief it was to discover that my self, my society, and my cosmos can be confirmed in their radical disparateness without that disparateness leading to quiet desperation or noisy anarchy" (p. ix).

Miller fails to see the validity of Niebuhr's correlation of the experience of the self as one with the idea of the self's god as one. In spite of his positive assessment of the many disparate centers of meaning that today function for a self, Miller still wants to speak of *the* self in *a* universe, whereas a radical polytheism according to Niebuhr's analysis would make any real unity of the self and of its universe impossible.

28. Niebuhr, "Faith in Gods and in God," p. 120.

29. Ibid., p. 122.

30. Though obviously his description of the radically monotheistic form of faith accords closely with the Christian, Niebuhr arrives at it by another route than by accepting revelation or adopting the tradition. He shows that the human need for faith is universal (an anthropological claim) and that the only kind of faith adequate to meet this universal human need is the radically monotheistic (since an adequate center of value must be infinite and one). As will be shown in chapter 6, the positive claims of Christian faith do not so much inform us about the character of the Infinite One; rather they enable us existentially to trust in and be loyal to that Infinite One.

31. Niebuhr, "The Center of Value," p. 113.

32. Ibid., p. 112–113.

33. Niebuhr, *The Responsible Self*, p. 44. Other instances of this type of metaphor are found when Niebuhr speaks of God as "the all-enveloping" ("The Triad of Faith," p. 12), as "the Omnipresence that is above, beneath, and about us" ("The Illusions of Power," *The Pulpit* 33 [April 1962]:7), and as "the circumambient being" ("The Ethical Crisis," *Universitas* 2 [Spring 1964]:48).

34. Niebuhr, *Radical Monotheism*, p. 38.

35. Paul Tillich, *Systematic Theology: Three Volumes in One* (Chicago: University of Chicago Press, 1967), 1:233–34.

36. See above, pp. 26–27.

37. Reinhold Niebuhr, "Must We Do Nothing?" *Christian Century* 49 (1932):417.

38. H. Richard Niebuhr, "A Communication: The Only Way into the Kingdom of God," *Christian Century* 49 (1932):447. Emphasis added.

39. H. Richard Niebuhr, "The Nature and Existence of God: A Protestant's View," *Motive* 4 (December 1943):13–15, 43–46. Niebuhr includes this piece with only minor stylistic revisions as one of the supplementary essays in his *Radical Monotheism and Western Culture* under the title "Faith in Gods and in God." Since the later version is more readily available I shall continue to refer to it rather than to the original.

40. Niebuhr, "Faith in Gods and in God," p. 122.

41. Niebuhr, "The Center of Value," p. 105, n. 1.

42. James W. Fowler recognizes in his analysis of Niebuhr's thought (*To See the Kingdom: The Theological Vision of H. Richard Niebuhr* [Nashville: Abingdon Press, 1974]) Niebuhr's debt to Tillich in the transitional years of his thinking from 1930–31 (pp. 61–67). However, Tillich's influence continues past those years to shape Niebuhr's formulation of this third way of speaking about the Infinite One.

43. Niebuhr, *Radical Monotheism*, p. 33, n. 7.

44. One is reminded here of the motto of Niebuhr's ethics of responsibility: "God is acting in all actions upon you. So respond to all actions upon you as to respond to his action." Niebuhr, *The Responsible Self*, p. 126.

45. Ibid., pp. 84, 85, 87.

46. Niebuhr, "Faith on Earth," chap. 3, p. 23,

47. Niebuhr, *Radical Monotheism*, p. 33.

48. Niebuhr uses "personal" as the adjective corresponding to the idea of "self" and not in the sense of "private."

49. Niebuhr, *Radical Monotheism*, p. 45.

50. All quotations in this paragraph are from *The Responsible Self*, pp. 84–85.

51. Even Jonathan Edwards, on whose thought Niebuhr's analysis of being heavily depends, realizes the difficulty of speaking in personal terms of that which is not personal. In his *Nature of True Virtue* (Ann Arbor: University of Michigan Press, Ann Arbor Paperbacks, 1960) Edwards proposes that "true virtue most essentially consists in *benevolence to being in general.* Or perhaps, to speak more accurately, it is that consent, propensity and union of heart to being in general, which is immediately exercised in a general good will" (p. 3). Niebuhr explicitly cites this idea of consent of being to being as theologically akin to his own view (in "The Center of Value," p. 105, n. 1). Yet Edwards qualifies what he means by "being in general" soon after he introduces the concept: "And perhaps it is needless for me to give notice to my readers, that when I speak of an intelligent being having a heart united and benevolently disposed to being in general, I thereby mean intelligent being in general. Not inanimate things, or beings that have no perception or will; which are not properly capable objects of benevolence" (p. 5).

52. Niebuhr, *Radical Monotheism*, pp. 86–87.

53. Richard Morrill also recognizes that Niebuhr's view fails to solve the problem of comparative value. See his "Selfhood and Value in Contemporary Protestant Ethics: A Constructive Analysis of the Theories of Roger Mehl and H. Richard Niebuhr" (Ph.D.

dissertation, Duke University, 1968). See also Thomas R. McFaul, "Dilemmas in H. Richard Niebuhr's Ethics," *Journal of Religion* 54 (January 1974):35–50.

54. H. Richard Niebuhr, *Christ and Culture* (New York: Harper & Row, Harper Torchbooks, 1956), p. 240.

55. All quotations from Niebuhr's lectures in the preceding paragraphs have been taken from Niebuhr's own lecture notes dated 28 April 1961.

56. Niebuhr, Christian Ethics Lectures 1952 (Yetter transcription), p. 116.

CHAPTER 5

1. Niebuhr, *The Responsible Self*, p. 48.

2. Ibid., pp. 52–53.

3. Ibid., p. 55.

4. Ibid.

5. Ibid., p. 59.

6. Niebuhr, "The Responsible Self" manuscript, chap. 2, pp. 12–14.

7. Niebuhr, *The Responsible Self*, p. 60.

8. Ibid., p. 56.

9. Readers familiar with *The Responsible Self* will be aware that this list of four elements differs slightly from the one in that book. There the four are (1) response, (2) interpretation, (3) accountability, and (4) social solidarity (pp. 61–65). I have chosen to present the list that appears in the Earl Lectures which Niebuhr delivered at the Pacific School of Religion in 1962 since it is a later version. Niebuhr appends social solidarity as a fifth element to this later list in the book manuscript "The Responsible Self" on which he was working at the time of his death.

10. H. Richard Niebuhr, The Earl Lectures, Pacific School of Religion, 1962, lecture 2, "The Meaning of Responsibility," p. 15. (Niebuhr manuscript collection.)

11. Ibid., p. 23.

12. Ibid., p. 26.

13. Ibid., pp. 28–29.

14. Niebuhr, "The Center of Value," p. 103.

15. Ibid.

16. Ibid.

17. See above, pp. 38–39.

18. Niebuhr, "The Responsible Self" manuscript, chap. 2, p. 21.

19. Ibid.

20. These analogies all appear in *The Responsible Self*, p. 97.

21. Ibid.

22. Niebuhr, "The Responsible Self" manuscript, chap. 2, p. 22.

23. Ibid., p. 23.

24. Ibid.

25. Ibid., pp. 22–23.

26. Ibid., p. 22. Cf. *The Responsible Self*, p. 108.

27. Niebuhr, *The Responsible Self*, pp. 108–9.

28. Ibid., pp. 60–61.

29. Niebuhr, "The Responsible Self" manuscript, chap. 2, p. 20. In a footnote to this passage Niebuhr indicates that he intended to address Stoic ethics more fully later in his book, and attached to this page in the manuscript is a scrap of paper on which he had listed several references that needed exploring with regard to the Greek idea of *kathēkonta*. Regrettably, he did not live to reach that point in his book.

30. Niebuhr, *The Responsible Self*, pp. 170–71.

31. For a more extensive treatment of the relation between Niebuhr's ethics of the fitting and Stoic ethics, see Richard E. Crouter, "H. Richard Niebuhr and Stoicism," *Journal of Religious Ethics* 2/2 (Fall 1974):129–46.

32. Niebuhr, *The Responsible Self*, p. 65.

33. George H. Mead, *Mind, Self, and Society from the Standpoint of a Social Behaviorist*, ed. Charles W. Morris (Chicago: University of Chicago Press, 1934), pp. 105–6. That Niebuhr's theory of the self is indebted to Mead's is a fact well-documented by both Niebuhr and the secondary literature on him; the more general question of Niebuhr's relation to Mead's social behaviorism has not, to my knowledge, been raised.

34. Niebuhr, *The Responsible Self*, p. 96.

35. I am indebted to Richard R. Niebuhr for this image. *Experiential Religion* (New York: Harper & Row, 1972), p. xiii.

36. Niebuhr, *The Responsible Self*, p. 101.

37. Ibid., pp. 105–6.

38. Niebuhr, "The Center of Value," p. 108.

39. Ibid., p. 103.

40. Ibid., p. 108.

41. Niebuhr, "The Responsible Self" manuscript, chap. 2, pp. 23–23b. See above, p. 135 n. 1.

42. Ibid., p. 24.

43. Ibid., pp. 26–27a. At the end of the just-quoted passage the following sentence is found: "In the theory of the moral life as fundamentally responsive and responsible the problem of the good receives as particular a formulation as does the problem of the right, but this subject we shall need to reserve for explicit discussion in the next chapter." Niebuhr died before the next chapter could be written.

44. This classificatory scheme is drawn from Richard B. Brandt's *Value and Obligation: Systematic Readings in Ethics* ([New York: Harcourt, Brace & World, 1961], pp. 249–56), but it is one that appears with only minor differences in William K. Frankena's *Ethics* (2nd. ed., Prentice-Hall Foundations of Philosophy Series [Englewood Cliffs, N. J.: Prentice-Hall, 1973], pp. 97–107). Frankena subsumes naturalism and supernaturalism under the more inclusive category of definist theories and uses the term intuitionism instead of nonnaturalism.

45. See above, chap. 3, sec. 2.

46. Niebuhr, "The Center of Value," p. 103.

47. Niebuhr, "Value-Theory and Theology," pp. 101, 110.

48. Niebuhr, *The Responsible Self*, pp. 124–25.

49. Niebuhr, "The Center of Value," p. 112.

50. I take up this topic more fully below in chapter 6.

51. These illustrations occur in *The Responsible Self*, pp. 108–9.

52. For this point I am indebted to Maurice Mandelbaum's *Phenomenology of Moral Experience* (Glencoe, Illinois: Free Press, 1955). Mandelbaum, like Niebuhr, uses the concept of fittingness as the basis for his analysis of moral judgments and suggests that it is a directly apprehended, phenomenally objective relational characteristic (pp. 60–61). He, also like Niebuhr, points to the meaning of the concept by appealing to examples that are not in themselves examples of moral fittingness. This leads him to observe that "the apprehended relation of fittingness which we have found to be basic to the presence of moral demands seems to be identical with apprehended fittingness in other cases." As a result he concludes: "That 'moral fittingness' should simply be an apprehended fittingness between a situation and an envisioned action, and not a unique type of fittingness at all, is a point of major theoretical importance. For if that which is the basis of a moral demand is not a uniquely moral fact, but an instance of a commonly experienced characteristic, then it may be said that our theory is 'naturalistic'" (p. 71).

Niebuhr at one point criticizes the value theory of the intuitionists. But he criticizes them not because they base their theory on intuition per se but because they make the intuition on which value is based unique to value alone. As a result of "having defined value as *sui generis*, distinct from existence, [they] tend almost inevitably it seems, to confuse it then with a certain kind of being, that of the ideas for instance, and at the same time to deny value to nonideal existence. They quickly confuse good with the idea of good and the latter with the goodness of ideas. The bifurcation between being and value becomes identified with the bifurcation of being into essence and existence, or of idea and power" (Niebuhr, "The Center of Value, p. 106). The bifurcation between being and value which intuitionism implies, not a general critique of intuition, constitutes the main thrust of Niebuhr's judgment.

53. Niebuhr, *The Responsible Self*, pp. 95–96.
54. Niebuhr, "The Center of Value," p. 106.
55. Niebuhr, *Radical Monotheism*, p. 13.
56. Niebuhr, "Faith on Earth," chap. 2, p. 49.
57. Cf. Arthur J. Dyck, "Moral Requiredness: Bridging the Gap between 'Ought' and 'Is'—Part II," *Journal of Religious Ethics* 9/1 (Spring 1981):131–150. Dyck views Niebuhr's theory as a theistic form of ideal observer theory and as a result classifies Niebuhr as a naturalist.

Jerry H. Gill also situates Niebuhr's thoughts on a metaethical spectrum, though he uses a different one than the above. See his "Christian Meta-Ethics? An Exploration of the Logical Status of the Judgments of the Christian Conscience," *Encounter* 29/2 (Spring 1968): 183–206.

58. Roderick Firth, "Ethical Absolutism and the Ideal Observer," *Philosophy and Phenomenological Research* 12/3 (March 1952):321.
59. Ibid., p. 319.
60. Ibid., p. 320.
61. Ibid., p. 324.
62. Ibid., pp. 333–345.
63. Ibid., p. 319.

64. For a discussion of the underlying objectivism in Niebuhr's view of value, see above, chap. 3.

65. Niebuhr, "The Center of Value," p. 103.

66. Niebuhr, *The Purpose of the Church and Its Ministry*, p. 20.

67. Niebuhr, *The Meaning of Revelation*, p. 65.

68. H. Richard Niebuhr, "Religion and Ethics," *The World Tomorrow* 13 (November 1930):445; *Christ and Culture*, p. 239; *The Responsible Self*, p. 88.

69. Niebuhr, "Faith in Gods and in God," p. 123.

70. Niebuhr, *The Responsible Self*, pp. 87–88. Firth also thinks that disinterest can be spoken of in a similar manner: "Now it seems to me that a large part of what we mean when we say an ideal judge is impartial, is that such a judge will not be influenced by interests of the kind which are commonly described as 'particular'—interests, that is to say, which are directed toward a particular person or thing but not toward other persons or things of the same kind." "Ethical Absolutism," p. 337.

71. Niebuhr, *The Meaning of Revelation*, p. 123.

72. Niebuhr, "The Center of Value," p. 108.

73. Niebuhr, "A Communication," p. 447.

74. Niebuhr, *The Meaning of Revelation*, p. 61.

CHAPTER 6

1. Niebuhr, "Value-Theory and Theology," p. 116.

2. Niebuhr, "Faith in Gods and in God," p. 117.

3. H. Richard Niebuhr, "The Ethics of Death" (Niebuhr manuscript collection).

4. Niebuhr, "Faith on Earth," chap. 4, p. 2.

5. Niebuhr, *The Responsible Self*, p. 109.

6. Niebuhr, "Faith on Earth," chap. 4, pp. 3–5.

7. Niebuhr, "Faith in Gods and in God," p. 122.

8. Niebuhr, "Faith on Earth," chap. 4, pp. 19, 23.

9. Niebuhr develops his analysis of sin as disloyalty in "Man the Sinner," *Journal of Religion* 15 (1935):272–80.

10. Niebuhr, "Faith on Earth," chap. 4, p. 23.

11. Ibid., p. 2.

12. Niebuhr, *The Responsible Self*, p. 45.

13. Niebuhr, *The Meaning of Revelation*, p. 133.

14. Ibid.

15. Niebuhr, *The Responsible Self*, p. 142.

16. Ibid.

17. Niebuhr, "Reformation: Continuing Imperative," p. 250.

18. Ibid.

19. Niebuhr, *The Meaning of Revelation*, p. 125.

20. H. Richard Niebuhr, "A Theologian's Approach to History: History's Role in Theology," an address for the American History Association, 1955 (Niebuhr manuscript collection), p. 4.

21. Niebuhr, "Faith in Gods and in God," pp. 123–24.

22. Niebuhr, *The Responsible Self*, p. 140.

23. Ibid., p. 44.

24. Ibid., p. 119.

25. Niebuhr, "Value-Theory and Theology," p. 114.

26. Niebuhr, *Radical Monotheism*, p. 89.

27. Niebuhr, "Value-Theory and Theology," p. 115.

28. Niebuhr, *The Meaning of Revelation*, p. 112.

29. Glowing words for Macintosh's empirical approach can be found in one of Niebuhr's early articles: "If theology would resolutely turn its back on all psychologism, if it would devote itself with the wholeheartedness which characterizes the natural sciences to the observation and intense study of its object as it is revealed in history and in the ethical and spiritual life, then it might eventually be found worthy of the name of science and its results might become as valuable for the religious life as the results of the natural sciences are for physical existence. Such a theology . . . has been set forth by Professor D. C. Macintosh." "Theology and Psychology: A Sterile Union," *Christian Century* 44 (1927):48. Lest these words be taken merely as a student's admiration of their thesis adviser, I point out that Niebuhr dedicated his *Meaning of Revelation* to Macintosh and another of his former teachers, Frank Chamberlain Porter, and said of them: "If the relation of my thought to their teaching is not always obvious to the reader, yet my dependence on them and on what I have learned from them is obvious to me." *The Meaning of Revelation*, p. xi.

30. Niebuhr, "Value-Theory and Theology," p. 95.

31. Ibid., p. 110.

32. Ibid., pp. 111–12.

33. Niebuhr makes the same point about his relation to liberalism in "Reformation: Continuing Imperative": "My fundamental break with the so-called liberal or empirical theology was not due to the fact that it emphasized human sovereignty; to interpret it in that way is to falsify it in unjustifiable fashion. It was rather due to the fact that it defined God primarily in value-terms, as the good, believing that good could be defined apart from God" (p. 248).

34. Niebuhr, *The Responsible Self*, p. 44.

35. Niebuhr, "Reformation: Continuing Imperative," p. 249. He expresses the same sentiment in *The Responsible Self*: "And for all this we are indebted to Jesus Christ, in our history, and in that depth of the spirit in which we grope with our theologies and theories of symbols. Could it have so happened otherwise; could the same results have been achieved through other means? That seems possible; nevertheless this one is our physician, this one is our reconciler to the Determiner of our Destiny" (p. 178).

36. Niebuhr, *Christ and Culture*, p, 254.

37. Niebuhr, *The Responsible Self*, p. 163.

38. Niebuhr, *Radical Monotheism*, p. 42.

39. Niebuhr, *The Responsible Self*, p. 164.

40. Ibid., pp. 175–76.

41. Ibid., pp. 176, 177. However one might describe Niebuhr's theology, his Christology is best described as liberal for three reasons: (1) The work of Christ is viewed as operative primarily in the experience of personal relationship to him. (2) Incarnation is discussed in terms of Christ's exemplifying radical faith and not in terms of his being God. And (3) what Christ changes is not the relation between God and the human but the human's perception of that relation. It is not that God was once our enemy and then through Christ became our friend; it is that we once interpreted God as our enemy and through Christ are able now to see God as friend.

42. Niebuhr, *The Responsible Self*, pp. 124–25.

43. H. Richard Niebuhr, "Science in Conflict with Morality?" *Radical Monotheism*, p. 137.

44. All quotations in this paragraph are taken from Niebuhr's own Christian Ethics lecture notes dated 26 April 1961.

45. Niebuhr, *Christ and Culture*, pp. 238–39.

46. Niebuhr, *Radical Monotheism*, pp. 32–33.

47. Niebuhr, "Faith on Earth," chap. 5, p. 21. See also *The Meaning of Revelation*, pp. 135–36.

48. Donald E. Fadner also recognizes that Niebuhr's identification of the principle of being and the principle of value is not consistently carried out. See *The Responsible God*, pp. 151–61.

49. Niebuhr, "Value-Theory and Theology," p. 116.

50. H. Richard Niebuhr, Review of *Systematic Theology, Volume I*, by Paul Tillich, in *Union Seminary Quarterly Review* 7 (November 1951):49.

51. Niebuhr, "Faith in Gods and in God," pp. 123–24.

52. Niebuhr, *The Responsible Self*, pp. 119, 123.

53. Niebuhr, *Radical Monotheism*, pp. 32–33.

54. Niebuhr, "Reformation: Continuing Imperative," p. 248. James Fowler confirms by his analysis of Niebuhr's works the centrality of this conception. See *To See the Kingdom*, pp. 53–95.

55. Niebuhr, "A Communication," p. 447.

56. Niebuhr, "Faith in Gods and in God," p. 122.

57. Niebuhr, "A Communication," p. 447.

58. To the best of my knowledge, Niebuhr never suggests that the interpretation of the ultimate context as inimical, as worthy of distrust is wrong, nor does he suggest that the interpretation of it as trustworthy, as good for what is, is right. What he does say is that one interpretation enables only distrust while the other enables trust. Since to live at all implicitly involves living in faith, and since faith in anything finite is ultimately to trust in something passing, then the way to have an unassailable vision of one's life is to put one's faith in that which is not passing: "We do not say that this faith in the last power is something men ought to have. We say only this, that it is the end of the road of faith, that it is unassailable, and when men receive it they receive a great gift." Niebuhr, "Faith in Gods and in God," p. 125.

59. Niebuhr, "Faith in Gods and in God," p. 123.

60. We do of course speak of love-hate relations. But we mean that we love certain aspects of a thing and hate other aspects, not that we both love and hate the identical aspect at the same time.

61. Niebuhr, "The Center of Value," p. 103.

62. Niebuhr here is simply following the traditional view of God's sovereignty and aseity.

63. Niebuhr, "The Center of Value," p. 112.

64. Niebuhr, "Value-Theory and Theology," p. 106.

65. Niebuhr, *The Responsible Self*, pp. 111–12.

66. Ibid., p. 119.

67. Ibid., p. 120.

68. See for example, *The Purpose of the Church and Its Ministry*, p. 36; "The Protestant Movement and Democracy in the United

States," in *The Shaping of American Religion*, ed. James Ward Smith and A. Leland Jamison (Princeton: Princeton University Press, 1961), p. 34; "Faith on Earth," chap. 4, p. 7; and *The Responsible Self*, p. 175.

69. H. Richard Niebuhr, "What Then Must We Do?" *Christian Century Pulpit* 5 (1934):147.

70. Niebuhr, "The Grace of Doing Nothing," p. 379.

71. H. Richard Niebuhr, "The Social Gospel in the Mind of Jesus," paper read before the American Theological Society, N.Y.C., 21 April 1933 (Niebuhr manuscript collection), pp. 11—12.

72. H. Richard Niebuhr, *The Gospel for a Time of Fears* (Washington: Henderson Services, 1950), p. 22.

73. Niebuhr, *The Responsible Self*, p. 173.

74. Ibid., pp. 164—65.

75. Donald E. Fadner also recognizes this ambiguity: "Niebuhr is grappling with the problem of how to hold together his conviction that God's continuous personal action in relation to his creatures is the one condition of the possibility of all acts, the one intention more or less adequately represented in all acts, with his conviction that how man responds to this action is crucial, that it makes a real objective difference in things whether he responds responsibly or irresponsibly. It doesn't really help, however, to suggest that God's action is not fatalistic because he is 'the loving dynamic One, who does new things,' unless what new things he does is at least partially determined by what new things we have done" (*The Responsible God*, p. 229). Fadner suggests that the way out of this dilemma, a way that Niebuhr himself failed to develop, is to think of God as a responsible self, interpreting alterations of God's creatures and making fitting responses to them.

CHAPTER 7

1. Niebuhr, "Value-Theory and Theology," p. 95.

2. Niebuhr, "The Center of Value," pp. 106—7.

3. Ibid., p. 113.

4. Niebuhr, "Value-Theory and Theology," p. 115.

5. Niebuhr, *The Meaning of Revelation*, p. 137.

6. Ibid., p. 135.

7. John B. Cobb, Jr., "Buddhist Emptiness and the Christian God," *Journal of the American Academy of Religion* 45/1 (March 1977):11.

Select Bibliography

I. WORKS BY H. RICHARD NIEBUHR

The following list of H. Richard Niebuhr's works draws heavily from the bibliographies compiled by (1) Raymond P. Morris and Jane E. McFarland in *Faith and Ethics: The Theology of H. Richard Niebuhr*, ed. Paul Ramsey (New York: Harper & Row, Harper Torchbooks, 1965), pp. 291–306; (2) James W. Fowler in his *To See the Kingdom: The Theological Vision of H. Richard Niebuhr* (Nashville: Abingdon Press, 1974), pp. 277–86; and (3) Michael Maeder in his "H. Richard Niebuhr's Doctrine of God and Critical Realism: An Attempt to Reconcile Orthodox Christianity with an Experiential View of God" (Ph.D dissertation, Graduate Theological Union, 1976), pp. 301–6.

A. PUBLISHED

The Advancement of Theological Education. With Williams, Daniel Day, and Gustafson, James M. New York: Harper & Bros., 1957.
"The Alliance between Labor and Religion." *Magazin für Evangelische Theologie und Kirche* 49 (1921):197–203.
"An Aspect of the Idea of God in Recent Thought." *Magazin für Evangelische Theologie und Kirche* 48 (1920): 39–44.
"The Attack upon the Social Gospel." *Religion in Life* 5 (1936): 176–81.
"An Attempt at a Theological Analysis of Missionary Motivation." *Occasional Bulletin from the Missionary Research Society* (New York) 14/1 (January 1963):1–6.
"Back to Benedict?" *Christian Century* 42 (1925):860–61.
"Booklist for Ministers." *Yale Divinity News* 34 (January 1938):2.

"Can German and American Christians Understand Each Other?"
Christian Century 47 (1930):914–16.

"The Center of Value." In *Moral Principles of Action: Man's Ethical
Imperative*, pp. 162–75. Edited by Ruth Nanda Anshen. Science
of Culture Series, vol. 5. New York: Harper & Bros., 1952. Revised and reprinted in H. Richard Niebuhr, *Radical Monotheism
and Western Culture: With Supplementary Essays*, pp. 100–113.
New York: Harper & Row, Harper Torchbooks, 1970.

Christ and Culture. New York: Harper & Row, 1951; Harper Torchbooks, 1956.

"The Christian Church in the World's Crisis." *Christianity and Society* 6/3 (1941):11–17.

Christian Ethics: Sources of the Living Tradition. Edited in conjunction with Beach, Waldo. New York: Ronald Press, 1955.

"The Christian Evangel and Social Culture." *Religion in Life* 8
(1939):44–49.

"Christianity and the Industrial Classes." *Theological Magazine of
the Evangelical Synod of North America* 57 (1929):12–18.

"Christianity and the Social Problem." *Magazin für Evangelische
Theologie und Kirche* 50 (1922):278–91.

The Church against the World. With Pauck, Wilhelm and Miller,
Francis P. Chicago: Willett, Clark, & Co., 1935. Niebuhr's contributions: "The Question of the Church," pp. 1–13; "Toward
the Independence of the Church," pp. 123–56.

The Churches and the Body of Christ. Philadelphia: Young Friends
Movement of the Philadelphia Yearly Meetings, 1953.

"The Churches and the Body of Christ." *Friends Intelligencer* 110
(1953):621–23.

"Churches That Might Unite." *Christian Century* 46 (1929):
259–61.

"A Communication: The Only Way into the Kingdom of God."
Christian Century 49 (1932):447.

"Critic's Corner." A reply to Willem F. Zuurdeeg. *Theology Today*
18 (1961):359–60.

"The Disorder of Man in the Church of God." In *Man's Disorder
and God's Design*, pp. 78–88. *The Universal Church in God's Design*,
vol 1. New York: Harper & Bros., 1949.

"The Doctrine of the Trinity and the Unity of the Church." *Theology Today* 3 (1946):371–84.

"The Ego-Alter Dialectic and the Conscience." *Journal of Philosophy* 42 (1945):352–59.

An Encyclopedia of Religion. S.v. "Church: Conceptions of the Church in Historic Christianity," "Ethics: Christian Ethics," "Inspiration," "Revelation," and "Troeltsch, Ernst." Edited by V. Ferm. New York: The Philosophical Library, 1945.

Encyclopedia of the Social Sciences. S.v. "Dogma," "Sectarian Education," "Fundamentalism," "Higher Criticism," "Protestantism," "Reformation: Non-Lutheran," "Religious Institutions, Christian: Protestant," "Schaff, Phillip," and "Sects." Edited by E. R. A. Seligman. New York: Macmillan Co., 1931.

"Ernst Troeltsch's Philosophy of Religion." Ph.D. dissertation, Yale University, 1924. Ann Arbor: University Microfilms, 1965.

"The Ethical Crisis." *Universitas* 2 (Spring 1964):41–50.

"Evangelical and Protestant Ethics." In *The Heritage of the Reformation: Essays Commemorating the Centennial of Eden Theological Seminary*, pp. 211–29. Edited by E .J. F. Arndt. New York: Richard R. Smith, 1950.

"Ex Libris." *Christian Century* 79 (1962):754.

"Faith, Works, and Social Salvation." *Religion in Life* 1 (1932): 426–30.

Foreword to *The Essence of Christianity*, by Ludwig Feuerbach. Translated by George Eliot. New York: Harper & Row, Harper Torchbooks, 1957. Pp. vii–ix.

Foreword to *In His Likeness*, by G. McLeod Bryan, pp. 5–6. Richmond: John Knox Press, 1959.

Foreword to *Self, Society, Existence*, by Paul Pfuetze. New York: Harper & Row, Harper Torchbooks, 1961.

"From the Religion of Humanity to the Religion of God." *Theological Magazine of the Evangelical Synod of North America* 57/6 (November 1929):401–9.

"The Gift of the Catholic Vision." *Theology Today* 4 (1948);507–21.

The Gospel for a Time of Fears. Washington: Henderson Services, 1950.

"The Grace of Doing Nothing." *Christian Century* 49 (1932): 378–80.

"The Hidden Church and the Churches in Sight." *Religion in Life* 15 (1945):106–17.

"The Idea of Covenant and American Democracy." *Church History* 23 (1954):126–35.

"The Illusions of Power." *The Pulpit* 33 (April 1962):4–7.

"Inconsistency of the Majority." *World Tomorrow* 17 (1934):43–44.

Introduction to *The Social Teachings of the Christian Churches*, by Ernst Troeltsch, pp. 7–12. New York: Harper & Row, Harper Torchbooks, 1960; reprint ed., Chicago: University of Chicago Press, Midway Reprints, 1976.

"The Irreligion of Communist and Capitalist." *Christian Century* 47 (1930):1306–7.

"Is God in the War?" *Christian Century* 59 (1942):953–55.

"Isolation and Co-operation in Theological Education." *Theological Education in America* (1955), no. 3, pp. 1–6.

"Issues between Catholics and Protestants at Midcentury." *Religion in Life* 23 (1954):199–205.

"Jesus Christ Intercessor." *International Journal of Religious Education* 3/4 (January 1927):6–8.

The Kingdom of God in America. Chicago: Willett, Clark, & Co., 1937; Harper & Row, Harper Torchbooks, 1959.

"Life is Worth Living." *Intercollegian and Far Horizons* 57 (1939): 3–4, 22.

"The Main Issues in Theological Education." With Williams, Daniel Day, and Gustafson, James M. *Theology Today* 11 (1955): 512–27.

"Man the Sinner." *Journal of Religion* 15 (1935):272–80.

The Meaning of Revelation. New York: Macmillan Publishing Co., 1941; Macmillan Paperbacks, 1960.

The Ministry in Historical Perspectives. Edited with Williams, Daniel Day. New York: Harper, 1956.

Moral Relativism and the Christian Ethic. New York: International Missionary Council, 1929.

"Nationalism, Socialism and Christianity." *World Tomorrow* 16 (1933):469–70.

"The Nature and Existence of God: A Protestant's View." *Motive* 4 (December 1943):13–15, 43–46. Revised and reprinted as "Faith in Gods and in God," in *Radical Monotheism and Western Culture*, pp. 114–26. New York: Harper & Row, Harper Torchbooks, 1970.

"The Norm of the Church." *Journal of Religious Thought* 4 (1946): 5–15.

"On the Nature of Faith." In *Religious Experience and Truth: A Sym-*

posium, pp. 93–102. Edited by Sidney Hook. New York: New York University Press, 1961.

"Participation in the Present Passion." *Pulpit Digest* 32 (September 1951):27–34.

"The Protestant Movement and Democracy in the United States." In *The Shaping of American Religion*, pp. 20–71. Edited by James Ward Smith and A. Leland Jamison. *Religion in American Life*, vol 1. Princeton: Princeton University Press, 1961.

The Purpose of the Church and Its Ministry: Reflections on the Aims of Theological Education. In collaboration with Williams, Daniel Day, and Gustafson, James M. New York: Harper & Bros., 1956; Harper & Row, Harper's Ministers Paperback Library, 1977.

Radical Monotheism and Western Culture: With Supplementary Essays. New York: Harper & Bros., 1960; Harper & Row, Harper Torchbooks, 1970.

"Reflections on Faith, Hope and Love." *Journal of Religious Ethics* 2/1 (1974):151–56.

"Reformation: Continuing Imperative." *Christian Century* 77 (March 1960):248–51.

"Religion and Ethics." *World Tomorrow* 13 (November 1930):443–46.

Die Religion in Geschichte und Gegenwart. S.v. "Emerson, Ralph Waldo (1803–82)"; "Individual- und Sozialethik." Third Edition. Edited by Hans von Campenhausen et al. Tübingen: J. C. B. Mohr (Paul Siebeck), 1959.

"Religious Realism in the Twentieth Century." In *Religious Realism*, pp. 413–28. Edited by D. C. Macintosh. New York: Macmillan Co., 1931.

"The Responsibility of the Church for Society." In *The Gospel, the Church and the World*, pp. 111–33. Edited by Kenneth Scott Latourette. The Interseminary Series, vol. 3. New York: Harper & Bros., 1946.

The Responsible Self: An Essay in Christian Moral Philosophy. Introduction by James M. Gustafson. New York: Harper & Row, 1963.

Review of *Beauty and Other Forms of Value*, by S. Alexander. *Yale Divinity News* 30 (January 1934):3.

Review of *Can We Keep the Faith?* by James Bissett Pratt. *Christendom* 6 (1941):591–92.

Review of *The Christian Doctrine of God. Dogmatics, Vol. 1*, by Emil Brunner. *Westminster Bookman* 9 (May–June 1950):3–4.

Review of *The Christian Philosophy of History*, by Shirley Jackson Case. *Journal of Religion* 24 (1944):147–48.

Review of *Christianity in America: A Crisis*, by E. G. Homrighausen. *Christian Century* 54 (1937):19–20.

Review of *Come, Holy Spirit*, by Karl Barth and Eduard Thurneysen. *Yale Divinity News* 31 (November 1934):4.

Review of *The Cross and the Eternal Order*, by Henry W. Clark. *Religion in Life* 15 (1946):314–15.

Review of *The Doctrine of Grace*, ed. by W. T. Whitley. *Crozer Quarterly* 9 (1932):475–76.

Review of *God in Idea and Experience, or The Apriori Elements of the Religious Consciousness*, by Rees Griffiths. *International Journal of Ethics* 43 (1932):91–93.

Review of *The Issues of Life*, by H. N. Wieman. *Yale Divinity News* 28 (November 1931):4.

Review of *Justice and the Social Order*, by Emil Brunner. *Theology Today* 3 (1947):558–60.

Review of *The Kingdom without End*, by Robert Elliot Fitch. *Religion in Life* 20 (1951):304–5.

Review of *The Misunderstanding of the Church*, by Emil Brunner. *Westminster Bookman* 12 (June 1953):11–13.

Review of *Pilgrimage of Faith in the Modern World*, by D. C. Macintosh. *Yale Divinity News* 28 (November 1931):3–4.

Review of *The Protestant Era*, by Paul Tillich. *Religion in Life* 18 (1949):291–92.

Review of *Redemption and Revelation in the Actuality of History*, by H. Wheeler Robinson. *Religion in Life* 12 (1943):463–64.

Review of *Säkulare Religion*, by Paul Schütz. *Anglican Theological Review* 14 (1932):359–61.

Review of *The Search for a New Strategy in Protestantism*, by Ivan Lee Holt. *Christendom* 1 (1936):877–78.

Review of *Sociology of Religion*, by Joachim Wach and *True Life: Sociology of the Supernatural*, by Luigi Sturzo. *Theology Today* 2 (1945):409–411.

Review of *Systematic Theology*, vol 1, by Paul Tillich. *Union Seminary Quarterly Review* 7 (November 1951):45–49.

Review of *Theology in Conflict*, by Gustaf Wingren. *Westminster Bookman* 18 (June 1959):2–4.

Review of *What is Christianity?* by Charles Clayton Morrison. *Journal of Religion* 21 (1941):189–92.

"Science and Religion" (a panel discussion with H. Richard Niebuhr, Liston Pope, Edgar Boell, Robert Calhoun, Henry Fairbank, and Ernest Pollard). *Yale Divinity News*, January 1960, pp. 3–21.

"The Seminary in the Ecumenical Age." *Theology Today* 17 (1960): 300–310. Originally appeared in *Princeton Seminary Bulletin* 54 (July 1960):38–45.

The Social Sources of Denominationalism. New York: Henry Holt & Co., 1929; reprint ed., New York: New American Library, Meridian Books, 1975.

"Some Books I Have Enjoyed Recently." *Yale Divinity News* 35 (February 1939):5.

"Soren Kierkegaard." In *Christianity and the Existentialists*, pp. 23–42. Edited by Carl Donald Michalson. New York: Scribners, 1956.

"Theology and Psychology: A Sterile Union." *Christian Century* 44 (1927):47–48.

"Theology—Not Queen but Servant." *Journal of Religion* 35 (1955): 1–5. Revised and reprinted as "Theology in the University," in *Radical Monotheism and Western Culture*, pp. 93–99.

"Towards a New Other-Worldliness." *Theology Today* 1 (1944): 78–87.

"Towards the Emancipation of the Church." *Christendom* 1 (1935): 133–45.

"Training a Preacher." *Presbyterian Survey* 46 (September 1956): 24–25.

Translator's Preface to *The Religious Situation*, by Paul Tillich. New York: Henry Holt & Co., pp. vii–xxii.

"The Triad of Faith." *Andover Newton Bulletin* 47 (October 1954): 3–12. (With corrigenda.)

"Two Lenten Meditations." *Yale Divinity News*, March 1939, pp. 3–4.

"Utilitarian Christianity." *Christianity and Crisis* 6/12 (July 1946): 3–5.

"Value-Theory and Theology." In *The Nature of Religious Experience: Essays in Honor of Douglas Clyde Macintosh*, pp. 93–116. Edited by Eugene Garrett Bewkes et al. New York: Harper & Bros., 1937.

"War as Crucifixion." *Christian Century* 60 (1943):513–15.

"War as the Judgment of God." *Christian Century* 59 (1942):630–33.

"What are the Main Issues in Theological Education?" *Theological Education in America*, 1954, no. 2, pp. 1–11.

"What Holds Churches Together?" *Christian Century* 43 (1926): 346–48.

"What Then Must We Do?" *Christian Century Pulpit* 5 (1934): 145–47.

"Who Are the Unbelievers and What Do They Believe?" In *The Christian Hope and the Task of the Church*, pp. 35–37. Six Ecumenical Surveys and the Report of the Assembly prepared by the Advisory Commission of the Main Theme, 1954. New York: Harper & Bros., 1954.

"Why Restudy Theological Education?" *Christian Century* 71 (1954):516–17, 527.

B. UNPUBLISHED

H. Richard Niebuhr's son, Richard R. Niebuhr of Harvard Divinity School, made available to me two file boxes of material, a portion of which is listed below. At the end of each entry I have indicated where the item is located in those boxes.

"An Academic Credo." Sermon preached at Vassar, 26 February 1961. 9 pp. (typewritten). Box 1, file 11.

"Address on Dr. Martin Buber's Eightieth Birthday." 1958. 10 pp. (handwritten). Box 1, file 7.

"The Alter-Ego Dialogue and Conscience." 8 pp. (mimeographed, with hand emendations). Box 2, file 2.

"American Religion: Its Roots and Fruits." Notes for two lectures at World Council Secretaries Conference, Lake Geneva, 17–21 June 1957. 12 pp. (handwritten). Box 2, file 7.

"The Anachronism of Jonathan Edwards." Address given in Northampton, Mass., on the bicentennial of Edward's death, 9 March 1958. 16 pp. (handwritten). Box 1, file 7.

"An Attempt at a Theological Analysis of Missionary Motivation." Written for Commission of International Missions, 16 April 1951. 11 pp. (typewritten). Box 2, file 3.

"Between Barth and Schleiermacher." 3 pp. (handwritten). Box 1, file 3-P-A.

"Between Past and Future." Sermon outline. 2 pp. (handwritten). Box 2, file 7.

"Chosen and Choosing." Sermon outline. 2 pp. (handwritten). Box 2, file 7.

Christian Ethics Lectures. Winter and Spring, 1952. Transcribed by Robert Yetter, Gene Canestrari, and Ed Elliot. 182 pp. (partly mimeographed, partly typewritten). Box 2, file 8.

Christian Ethics Lectures: Outlines and Notes. 1961. 239 pp. (handwritten). Box 1, file 10.

"A Christian Interpretation of War." For Federal Council of Churches, 1943. 10 pp. (mimeographed). Box 2, file 3.

"The Church Defines Itself in the World." 1958. 15 pp. (typewritten). Box 1, file 6.

"Conscience: Its Role in Ethics and Religion." Paper read at American Theological Society, N.Y.C., 7 April 1945. 18 pp. (typewritten). Box 2, file 2.

"The Consoling Thought of Divine Judgment." Sermon preached at Connecticut College for Women, Wellesey College, and Penn State. Winter, 1954. 9 pp. (partly handwritten, partly typewritten). Box 1, file 11.

"The Definition of Man." Baccalaureate sermon, University of North Carolina. 31 May 1959. 9 pp. (carbon with handwritten emendations). Box 2, file 3.

"Doubting Believers and Believing Doubters." Sermon preached at Spring Glen Church. 28 April 1957. 5 pp. (handwritten). Box 2, file 2.

"The Ethics of Death." 2 pp. (typewritten with hand emendations). Box 1, file 5-A.

"The Ethics of Survival." Sermon outline. College Church of the Claremont Colleges, 4 March 1962. 3 pp. (handwritten). Box 2, file 3.

"Faith on Earth: An Inquiry into the Structure of Faith." Book Manuscript. N.d. 1. "Faith in Question," 24 pp.; 2. "Believing and Knowing in Community," 15 pp.; 3. "The Structure of Faith," 23 pp.; 4. "Broken Faith," 23 pp.; 5. "The Reconstruction of Faith," 22 pp.; 7. "The Community of Faith," 19 pp. (typewritten with handwritten emendations). [Note: Chapter numbers are not clear. Niebuhr has renumbered the manuscript at least twice. There is no chapter 6.] Box 1, file 3-B.

"Faith, Reason, Feeling, Valuing." 6 pp. (typewritten with hand-written emendations). Box 1, 3-P-A.

"Freedom and Our Calling." Sermon. Newton, Mass. 16 October 1949. 6 pp. (typewritten). Box 2, file 2.

"From Doubt of Man to Faith in Being." Baccalaureate sermon, Wesleyan University. 10 June 1956. 8 pp. (handwritten). Box 2, file 7.

"Going Home." Sermon preached at North Cornwall, 19 August 1951. 7 pp. (handwritten). Box 1, file 11.

"The Grand Line of the Church in the World." Unfinished. 11 pp. Box 2, file 3.

"The Hope of Glory." Sermon. Box 1, file 11.

"The Idea of Original Sin in American Culture." Paper read before the Princeton University Program of Studies in American Civilization, 24 February 1949. 28 pp. (handwritten). Box 1, file 12.

"In Quietness and Confidence." Address delivered at Elmhurst Commencement. 1955. 5 pp. (handwritten). Box 2, file 2.

"Is There an American Church?" An address. 1955. Box 1, file 6.

"Kingdom of God and Eschatology (Social Gospel and Barthian-ism)" 4 pp. (mimeographed). Box 2, file 2.

"Knowledge of Faith." Book Manuscript. 1. "Faith Seeks Under-standing," 32 pp.; 2. "Towards Understanding Understanding," 24 pp.; 3. "Faith is a Relation between Selves," 30 pp.; 4. "The Trialectic of Faith," 41 pp. (typewritten). Box 1, file 1-A.

"Life on the Boundary." Commencement address, Garrett Biblical Institute. 16 June 1952. 14 pp. (handwritten). Box 2, file 7.

"The Limitation of Power and Religious Liberty." Address delivered at the Institute of Human Relations. Williamstown, Mass. 27 August 1939. 16 pp. (typewritten). Box 1, file 12.

"Living Tradition in Theology." Address at Hartford Seminary. October 1956. 8 pp. (handwritten). Box 2, file 7.

"The Logic of the Cross." Sermon. 10 pp. (typewritten).

"The Lord's Prayer." Sermon delivered at Union Theological Seminary. 1953. Transcription from recording. 9 pp. (typewrit-ten). Box 2, file 3.

"Man's Word to God." Sermon. Union Theological Seminary. 6 pp. (handwritten). Box 1, file 11.

"Man's Work and God's." Sermon. 9 pp. (typewritten). Box 1, file 11.

"Martin Luther and the Renewal of Human Confidence." Address at the centennial of the founding of Valparaso University. 1959. 21 pp. (typewritten). Box 1, file 7.

"The Nature of Faith." The Swander Lectures. The Theological Seminary of the Evangelical and Reformed Church. Lancaster, Pennsylvania. 13–15 November 1950. 1. "Faith in Question"; 2. "The Threefold Bond"; 3. "The Community of Faith"; 4. "The Mediation of Faith." (Handwritten and typewritten, much in outline form.) Box 1, files 5-A, 5-B.

"The Norm of the Christian Character of the Church." 13 pp. (mimeographed). Box 1, file 6.

"The Old Time Religion Isn't Good Enough." Sermon preached at Connecticut College. 25 October 1959. 10 pp. (handwritten). Box 2, file 2.

"On Being Found." Sermon outline. 2 pp. (handwritten). Box 2, file 7.

"On the Meaning of Responsibility." Lecture delivered at Cambridge University. 25 May 1960 21 pp. (handwritten). Box 2, file 1.

"Our Reverent Doubt and the Authority of Christ." Anniversary sermon, Yale Divinity School. 6 June 1948. 9 pp. (carbon). Box 2, file 2.

"The Pathology of Unbelief." 27 pp. (handwritten). Box 1, file 2.

"The Preacher's Poverty and the Unsearchable Riches of Christ." Sermon preached at the ordination of Richard R. Niebuhr. Cornwall, Connecticut. 26 November 1950. Box 2, file 2.

"Protestantism and Democracy In America." Outlines for three lectures. 22–23 January 1958. 10 pp. (handwritten). Box 2, file 7.

"The Reason in Faith and the Faith in Reason." Convocation address, Associated Colleges, Claremont, California. 14 November 1957. 6 pp. (handwritten). Box 1, file 3-AP.

"Reconciliation to Being." Sermon outline. 3 pp. (handwritten). Box 2, file 7.

"Reflections on a 'Protestant Theory of Higher Education.'" 3 pp. (typewritten). Box 2, file 4.

"The Reformers' Ideal of a Church in the World." Paper read at Western section, World Alliance of Presbyterian Churches. Albany, New York. 1939. 15 pp. (typewritten). Box 1, file 6.

"The Relation of Christianity and Democracy." The Earl Lecture.

Berkeley Divinity School. October 1940. 23 pp. (typewritten). Box 2, file 3.

"Pt. II. Responsibility to Divine Action; I. Valuation." Fragment. 13 pp. (handwritten). Box 2, file 4.

"The Responsible Self." The Earl Lectures at Pacific School of Religion. [1962] 1. "Metaphors and Morals," 21 pp. (carbon); 2. "The Meaning of Responsibility," 30 pp. (typewritten); 3. "Responsibility to God or Universal Responsibility," 20 pp. (partly typewritten, partly handwritten). Box 2, file 1.

"The Responsible Self" manuscript. Drafts of two chapters for projected book. [Found on Niebuhr's desk at time of his death.] 1. "Metaphors and Morals," 41 pp. (typewritten); 2. "The Meaning of Responsibility," 34 pp. + numerous addenda (typewritten). Box 2, file 6.

"The Shape of Things to Come." Baccalaureate sermon. Connecticut College, New London. 5 June 1943. 7 pp. (carbon). Box 2, file 3.

"Der Sinn der Verantwortlichkeit." Lecture delivered at Bonn. 28 June 1960. 20 pp. (typewritten). Box 2, file 1.

"The Social Gospel and the Mind of Jesus." Paper read at meeting of the American Theological Society, N.Y.C. 21 April 1933. Box 1, file 7.

"The Spirit That Lives in Us and in Which We Live." Sermon preached at Vassar College Chapel. 17 May 1953. 5 pp. (handwritten). Box 1, file 11.

"Strangers to Ourselves." Sermon outline. 2 pp. (handwritten). Box 2, file 7.

"The Symbol of Structure." 2 pp. (handwritten). Box 1, file 3-P-A.

"A Theologian's Approach to History: History's Role in Theology." An address to the American History Association. Washington. 30 December 1955. 7 pp. (partly typewritten, partly handwritten). Box 2, file 3.

"Theological Frontiers." The Cole Lectures, Vanderbilt University, 1960. Four lectures transcribed from tape recording by Typewritten Transcription, Co. 1. "The Position of Theology Today," 21 pp.; 2. "Towards New Symbols," 30 pp.; 3. "Towards the Recovery of Feeling," 30 pp.; 4. "Toward the Service of Christendom," 33 pp. (typewritten.) Box 2, file 5.

"Theology and the Critique of the Christian Life." Address given at the meeting of the Association of Seminary Professors of Social Ethics. Philadelphia. 31 January 1958. 14 pp. (handwritten). Box 2, file 4.

"Theology in a Time of Disillusionment." Alumni lecture, Yale Divinity School, 1931. 22 pp. (handwritten). Box 1, file 7.

"Theology of Education." An address at the Week of Work of the National Council on Religion in Higher Education. 1953. Transcribed by the Master Reporting Co. 14 pp. (typewritten). Box 2, file 4.

"Threat and Promise in Our Crisis." Three versions. 16 pp., 7 pp., 10 pp. (all handwritten). Box 2, file 3.

"Types of Christian Ethics." 1942. 9 pp. (mimeographed). Box 2, file 2.

Untitled essay on the Kingdom Gospel and other-worldliness, 1919. 6 pp. (typewritten). Box 2, file 3.

Untitled introductory remarks for lectures on faith. 1 p. (handwritten). Box 2, file 7.

"When the Half-Gods Go." Sermon outline. 5 pp. (handwritten). Box 2, file 7.

"Who are the Unbelievers and What Do They Believe?" Paper written for Commission on Evangelism, World Council of Churches. Summer, 1953. 10 pp. (carbon). Box 1, file 11.

"The Wisdom of Survival and the Logic of the Cross." Sermon. 8 pp. (handwritten). Box 1, file 11.

II. WORKS ABOUT H. RICHARD NIEBUHR

The following sources are either wholly or in part directed to criticism of H. Richard Niebuhr's thought.

Ahlstrom, Sidney E. "H. Richard Niebuhr's Place in American Thought." *Christianity and Crisis* 23 (1963):213–17.

Allen, Joseph L. "A Decisive Influence on Protestant Ethics." *Christianity and Crisis* 23 (1963):217–19.

Cauthen, Kenneth. "An Introduction to the Theology of H. Richard Niebuhr." *Canadian Journal of Theology* 10 (1964):4–14.

Chrystal, William G. "The Young H. Richard Niebuhr." *Theology Today* 38 (1981):231–35.

Cobb, John B., Jr. *Living Options in Protestant Theology*. Philadelphia: Westminster Press, 1962.

Crouter, Richard E. "H. Richard Niebuhr and Stoicism." *Journal of Religious Ethics* 2/2 (Fall 1974):129–46.

Dyck, Arthur J. "Moral Requiredness: Bridging the Gap Between 'Ought' and 'Is'—Part II." *Journal of Religious Ethics* 9/1 (Spring 1981):131–150.

Fadner, Donald E. *The Responsible God: A Study of the Christian Philosophy of H. Richard Niebuhr.* American Academy of Religion Dissertation Series, no. 13. Missoula, Montana: Scholars Press, 1975.

Ferre, Nels F. S. "The Revelatory Moment within Christian Faith." Review of *The Meaning of Revelation. Christendom* 6 (1941): 439–41.

Fowler, James W. "H. Richard Niebuhr as Philosopher: Fadner's *The Responsible God.*" *Journal of Religion* 57 (July 1977): 307–13.

———. *To See the Kingdom: The Theological Vision of H. Richard Niebuhr.* Nashville: Abingdon Press, 1974.

Furr, W. Hal. "An Introduction to the Thought of H. Richard Niebuhr." Ph.D. dissertation, Temple University, 1971. Ann Arbor: University Microfilms, 71-31079.

Gill, Jerry H. "Christian Meta-Ethics?" *Encounter* 29/2 (Spring 1968):183–206.

Gustafson, James. "Context Versus Principles: A Misplaced Debate in Christian Ethics." *Harvard Theological Review* 58 (1965): 171–202.

Hamilton, Kenneth. "Trinitarianism Disregarded: The Theological Orientation of H. Richard Niebuhr." *Encounter* 23 (1962): 343–52.

Harvey, Van A. *The Historian and the Believer.* New York: Macmillan Co., 1966.

Hoedemaker, Libertus A. *The Theology of H. Richard Niebuhr.* Foreword by James M. Gustafson. Philadelphia: Pilgrim Press, 1970.

Irish, Jerry A. *The Religious Thought of H. Richard Niebuhr.* Atlanta: John Knox Press, 1983.

Kliever, Lonnie D. "The Christology of H. Richard Niebuhr." *Journal of Religion* 50 (1970):33–57.

———. *H. Richard Niebuhr.* Makers of the Modern Theological Mind. Waco, Texas: Word Books, 1977.

Koops, Hugh A. "The Christening of Ethics: A Structural Analysis of the Criteria of Value in the Moral Reflection of H. Richard Niebuhr." Ph.D. dissertation, University of Chicago, 1972.

Kuhn, Helmut. "Conscience and Society." *Journal of Religion* 26 (July 1946):203–14.

Loomer, Bernard M. "Neo-Naturalism and Neo-Orthodoxy." *Journal of Religion* 28 (1948):79–91.

McFaul, Thomas R. "Dilemmas in H. Richard Niebuhr's Ethics." *Journal of Religion* 54 (January 1974):35–50.

Macintosh, D. C. "Theology, Valuational or Existential?" *Review of Religion* 4 (1939):23–44.

Maeder, Michael. "H. Richard Niebuhr's Doctrine of God and Critical Realism: An Attempt to Reconcile Orthodox Christianity with an Experiential View of God." Ph.D. dissertation, Graduate Theological Union, 1976.

Miller, David L. *The New Polytheism: Rebirth of the Gods and Goddesses.* New York: Harper & Row, 1974.

Morrill, Richard Leslie. "Selfhood and Value in Contemporary Protestant Ethics: A Constructive Analysis of the Theories of Roger Mehl and H. Richard Niebuhr." Ph.D. dissertation, Duke University, 1968.

Niebuhr, Reinhold. "Must We Do Nothing?" *Christian Century* 49 (1932):415–17.

Ottati, Douglas F. *Meaning and Method in H. Richard Niebuhr's Theology.* Washington: University Press of America, 1982.

Ramsey, Paul, ed. *Faith and Ethics: The Theology of H. Richard Niebuhr.* New York: Harper & Row, 1957; Harper Torchbooks, 1965.

———. *Nine Modern Moralists.* Englewood Cliffs, N. J.: Prentice-Hall, 1962.

Sandon, Leo., Jr. "H. Richard Niebuhr's Interpretation of the American Theological Tradition." Ph.D. dissertation, Boston University, 1971.

Shinn, Roger. Review of *Radical Monotheism,* by H. Richard Niebuhr. *Interpretation* 16/2 (1962):197–199.

Thomas, George F. Review of *The Meaning of Revelation,* by H. Richard Niebuhr. *Journal of Religion* 21 (1941):455–60.

Tillich, Paul. "Existential Thinking in American Theology." Review of *The Meaning of Revelation. Religion in Life* 10 (1941): 452–55.

Van Dusen, H. P. Introduction to *The Christian Answer.* Edited by H. P. Van Dusen. New York: Chas. Scribner's Sons, 1945. Pp. vii–xi.

Williams, Daniel Day. Review of *Radical Monotheism*. *Union Seminary Quarterly Review* 17/1 (1961):99–101.
Yeager. D. M. "On Making the Tree Good: An Apology for a Dispositional Ethics." *Journal of Religious Ethics* 10/1 (Spring 1982):103–120.

III. OTHER WORKS

Adams, James Luther. *Paul Tillich's Philosophy of Culture, Science and Religion*. New York: Schocken Books, Schocken Paperbacks, 1970.
Brandt, Richard B. *Value and Obligation: Systematic Readings in Ethics*. New York: Harcourt, Brace & World, 1961.
Cobb, John B., Jr. "Buddhist Emptiness and the Christian God." *Journal of the American Academy of Religion* 45/1 (March 1977): 11–25.
Collingwood, R. G. *An Essay on Metaphysics*. Oxford: Clarendon Press, 1940.
Edwards, Jonathan. *The Nature of True Virtue*. Ann Arbor: University of Michigan Press, Ann Arbor Paperbacks, 1960.
Firth, Roderick. "Ethical Absolutism and the Ideal Observer." *Philosophy and Phenomenological Research* 12 (1952): 317–45.
Frankena, William K. *Ethics*. Second edition. Prentice-Hall Foundations of Philosophy Series. Englewood Cliffs, N. J.: Prentice-Hall, 1973.
Kant, Immanuel. *Critique of Practical Reason*. Translated, with an Introduction, by Lewis White Beck. The Library of Liberal Arts. Indianapolis: Bobbs-Merrill, 1956.
———. *Critique of Pure Reason*. Unabridged edition. Translated by Norman Kemp Smith. New York: St. Martin's Press, 1965 [1929].
Lewis, C. I. *An Analysis of Knowledge and Valuation*. The Paul Carus Lectures, series 8, 1946. La Salle, Illinois: Open Court, 1946.
Mandelbaum, Maurice. *The Phenomenology of Moral Experience*. Glencoe, Illinois: Free Press, 1955.
Mead, George H. *Mind, Self, and Society from the Standpoint of a Social Behaviorist*. Edited, with an Introduction, by Charles W. Morris. Chicago: University of Chicago Press, 1934.
Niebuhr, Richard R. *Experiential Religion*. New York: Harper & Row, 1972.

Perry, Ralph Barton. *General Theory of Value: Its Meaning and Basic Principles Construed in Terms of Interest.* New York: Longmans, Green & Co., 1926.

Royce, Josiah. *The Philosophy of Loyalty.* New York: Macmillan Co., 1908.

Tillich, Paul. *The Protestant Era.* Abridged edition. Translated by James Luther Adams. Chicago: University of Chicago Press, Phoenix Books, 1957.

Toulmin, Stephen. *An Examination of the Place of Reason in Ethics.* Cambridge: Cambridge University Press, 1950.

Index